P9-DTX-499

MVFOL

A HISTORICAL READER

THE *Atomic*
Bomb

nextext

Cover photograph: CORBIS/BETTMANN

Printed in the United States of America
ISBN 0-395-98665-6

1 2 3 4 5 6 7 — QKT — 06 05 04 03 02 01 00

Table of Contents

*Throughout the reader, vocabulary words appear in boldface
type and are footnoted. Specialized or technical words and phrases
appear in lightface type and are footnoted.*

Development of the Bomb

Albert Einstein's Letter to President Roosevelt

The United States' effort to build an atomic bomb began in 1939 with a letter from Albert Einstein to President Franklin Roosevelt. Albert Einstein was the world's most famous scientist. He had emigrated to the United States in the 1930s, fleeing from the Nazi government in Germany. The physicist Leo Szilard, who had been working on fission and the possibility of a nuclear chain reaction, enlisted Einstein's aid to warn the U.S. government of the newly discovered danger of the atomic bomb. At Szilard's prompting, Einstein wrote a letter to President Roosevelt detailing the danger and making some recommendations.

Albert Einstein
Old Grove Rd.
Nassau Point
Peconic, Long Island

August 2nd, 1939

F. D. Roosevelt,
President of the United States,
White House
Washington, D.C.

Sir:

Some recent work by E. Fermi and L. Szilard,[1] which has been communicated to me in manuscript, leads me to expect that the element uranium may be turned into a new and important source of energy in the immediate future. Certain aspects of the situation which has arisen seem to call for watchfulness and, if necessary, quick action on the part of the Administration. I believe therefore that it is my duty to bring to your attention the following facts and recommendations:

In the course of the last four months it has been made probable—through the work of Joliot in France as well as Fermi and Szilard in America—that it may become possible to set up a nuclear chain reaction in a large mass of uranium, by which vast amounts of power and large quantities of new radium-like elements would be generated. Now it appears almost certain that this could be achieved in the immediate future.

This new phenomenon would also lead to the construction of bombs, and it is conceivable—though much less certain—that extremely powerful bombs of a new

---

[1] E. Fermi and L. Szilard—physicists who created the first nuclear chain reaction.

type may thus be constructed. A single bomb of this type, carried by boat and exploded in a port, might very well destroy the whole port together with some of the surrounding territory. However, such bombs might very well prove to be too heavy for transportation by air.

The United States has only very poor ores of uranium in moderate quantities. There is some good ore in Canada and the former Czechoslovakia, while the most important source of uranium is Belgian Congo.

In view of this situation you may think it desirable to have some permanent contact maintained between the Administration and the group of physicists working on chain reactions in America. One possible way of achieving this might be for you to entrust with this task a person who has your confidence and who could perhaps serve in an inofficial capacity. His task might comprise the following:

a) to approach Government Departments, keep them informed of the further development, and put forward recommendations for Goverment action, giving particular attention to the problem of securing a supply of uranium ore for the United States;

b) to speed up the experimental work, which is at present being carried on within the limits of the budgets of University laboratories, by providing funds, if such funds be required, through his contacts with private persons who are willing to make contributions for this cause, and perhaps also by obtaining the co-operation of industrial laboratories which have the necessary equipment.

I understand that Germany has actually stopped the sale of uranium from the Czechoslovakian mines which she has taken over. That she should have taken such early action might perhaps be understood on the ground that the son of the German Under-Secretary of State, von Weizsäcker, is attached to the Kaiser-Wilhelm-Institut in Berlin where some of the American work on uranium is now being repeated.

Yours very truly,

(Albert Einstein)

QUESTIONS TO CONSIDER

1. What is Einstein's purpose in writing to Roosevelt?

2. In your opinion, how accurate were Einstein's concerns about the power and weight of the bomb?

3. Who does Einstein view as the serious threat to use atomic power?

The ABC
of the Atom

BY J. BRONOWSKI

*J. Bronowski was a British physicist who also worked as a writer,
trying to increase the general public's understanding of modern
science. "The ABC of the Atom" is an explanation of the physics
of nuclear weapons for a general audience. It was written for*
Hiroshima Plus 20, *a book published by* The New York Times
*in 1967, which examined the controversies and legacy of the use
of the atomic bomb.*

Men have been talking about the atom now, off and
on, for 2,000 years. Yet to this day nobody has ever seen
an atom; until about 35 years ago nobody had seen anything which even resembled an atom. Then why have
we been so sure, all these 2,000 years, that the atom was
there, somewhere at the heart of matter, if only we could
find it?

The reason, oddly, has little to do with scientific experiment and finesse. It is a solid logical reason which remains as plain today as it was to the Greeks who first thought of it. If I put a lump of salt on my tongue, I know at once what it is: it tastes salt. If I crumble the lump into grains and taste only a grain, I still know it to be salt. If I put the grain under the microscope and pick it apart into its tiny crystals, each crystal is still salt and nothing else. We can shatter the little glittering crystal into smaller crystals; the process of breaking can go on and on; but it is not conceivable that it can go on forever.

There must be a smallest unit of salt beyond which we cannot go if we want still to have salt. There must be a tiniest unit of sugar which remains sugar, and in the same way there must be characteristic units of every substance—iron and the green chlorophyll in leaves, and pencil lead and vitamin B_{12}. A patient may be cured of pernicious anemia by as little as a millionth of an ounce of vitamin B_{12}. But still there must be a smallest piece of the vitamin which makes it B_{12}.

This is the picture of matter which we have had since the Greeks. A substance is made up of tiny pieces, each of them itself **indivisible**,[1] each alike, and each characteristic of that substance and not something else. The Greeks called these pieces atoms, which means "indivisible."

It is important to begin this way, historically and logically. For this makes us aware that our idea of an atom starts from common sense; it is based on everyday notions and experiences which we all share. Of course, we have to go on from these to more modern and detailed conceptions. But even those, we must remember, are attempts to find simplicity and order in the bewildering variety of natural substances. Never believe that the atom is a complex mystery—it is not. The atom is what

---

[1] **indivisible**—not capable of being divided into smaller parts.

we find when we look for the underlying architecture in nature, whose bricks are as few, as simple and as orderly as possible.

With that, we are ready to begin our questioning of nature.

An atom is the smallest piece of an elementary substance which is characteristic of that substance and not something else.

This is still the Greek answer, but we have narrowed it by adding one word—the word "elementary." The Greeks only thought of cutting up a lump of salt physically. We have learned in the last 150 years that it can also be taken apart chemically, reduced to two more elementary substances, **sodium**[2] and **chlorine**.[3] Therefore nowadays we distinguish between compound substances, which can be taken apart chemically, and elementary substances, which cannot. We reserve the word "atom" for the smallest unit of one of these elementary substances.

There are about 100 different elementary substances, and therefore about 100 different kinds of atoms. Yet all these atoms—whether of hydrogen or oxygen, carbon or gold or **uranium**[4]—are put together from the same smaller parts.

Every substance is built up of atoms, either all of one kind or a linked arrangement of several kinds. Therefore, atoms are found everywhere where there is matter.

In a solid, atoms are arranged tidily. When the solid melts into a liquid the atoms wander from their neat stations, but they are not lost. And when the liquid boils up into a gas the atoms dart about and take up more and more space. But the atoms are still there, everywhere, in solid, liquid and gas.

---

[2] **sodium**—a light, highly reactive element that is easily combined, as in salt.

[3] **chlorine**—an element capable of combining with almost all other elements.

[4] **uranium**—element often used in nuclear fuels.

The air in your lungs at this instant is made up of atoms—about 10,000,000,000,000,000,000,000 of them. This will do as a figure to end all figures. It is, for example, a good deal more than the number of cells in the brains and bodies of all the nearly three billion inhabitants of the world today, added together.

In what way do the atoms vary one from another?

Seventy years ago we had no idea. Each kind of atom was permanent, indivisible and different from every other; that was all we knew. Only since then have we discovered, slowly, step by step, and with mounting astonishment, that under this variety lies a deeper unity. Nature, which has built its wealth of compounds, rocks and proteins, ores and sugars and living bones, all from only 100 atoms—nature has a still more profound economy. For each atom itself has a structure—and a much simpler structure.

All atoms are assembled from three kinds of fundamental electrical **particles**.[5] They are the proton (electrically positive), the neutron (electrically neutral) and the electron (electrically negative).

It would be elegant if these fundamental particles were all equally heavy, but they are not. The proton and the neutron are heavy particles—each has almost 2,000 times the mass of an electron—but even they are not quite equal. And the electron is so light that it really seems to be nothing but a tiny charge of negative electricity.

Atoms vary only in the number of fundamental particles from which they are assembled. Every kind of atom has essentially the same structure. At the center there is a heavy kernel or nucleus in which all the heavy particles in the atom are concentrated. Away on the outskirts of the atom are the light electrons.

The electrons are in constant movement. They circle around the nucleus much as the planets circle around

---

[5] **particles**—very small pieces or parts.

the sun. But their orbits are less precise, so that they form a kind of spinning cloud or shell.

In fact, the electrons are only the outriders of the atom. They are lost and recovered, they wander off in an electric current, but still the atom remains essentially the same. For the solid substance and anchor of the atom is its heavy nucleus.

The nucleus is made up of protons and neutrons, tightly bound together. Their numbers are characteristic of each kind of atom. In particular, each elementary substance has a characteristic number of protons in its atoms. The nucleus of hydrogen has one proton, the nucleus of helium has two, and so on up the scale of nature to uranium, whose nucleus has 92 protons. Beyond this lie the new elements which man has created in the atomic pile—neptunium, with a nucleus of 93 protons; plutonium, with 94, and higher still.

The atom of ordinary hydrogen has only a proton for its nucleus and, to balance its electric charge, one electron circling around it. The atom of helium has a nucleus of two protons and two neutrons bound together; their electric charge is balanced by two electrons which circle around the nucleus at a distance.

The nucleus of explosive uranium is made up of 92 protons and 143 neutrons, and by way of electrical balance there are, on an average, 92 electrons circling on the outskirts of this atom.

The picture of an atom of ordinary uranium would be the same, except that there would be three more neutrons in the center. For the two kinds of uranium are merely variants or **isotopes**[6] of the same element, and isotopes differ by a few neutrons but nothing else.

For example, even the nucleus of hydrogen may have an extra neutron. This makes the atom into heavy hydrogen, which is a variant or isotope of hydrogen.

---

[6] **isotope**—one of two or more atoms that have the same atomic number but different mass numbers.

The structure of the atom is held together by invisible forces. For example, there is an electrical attraction between the positive nucleus and the negative electrons. But this is a modest force, no more violent than that with which our sun holds the planets in their orbits.

The greater energy lies like a coiled spring in the nucleus itself. For the nucleus is full of protons which are all electrically positive, and which ought therefore to repel one another with enormous forces. Somehow these electrical forces are held in check; an unknown binding energy which we do not understand welds the protons and the neutrons into a single stable kernel.

Therefore, atomic energy is nuclear energy. It is the binding energy which holds the nucleus together, and checks the electrical repulsions which would make it fly violently apart.

The nucleus of every atom is very stable. But some of the heavier atoms are unstable and, from time to time, fire off a part of the nucleus of their own accord. These are the naturally radioactive atoms, such as radium and uranium. In them, the nucleus tries to simplify itself spontaneously to a more stable form. For the most stable nucleus is neither among the very light nor the very heavy elements, but about halfway between.

Whenever a nucleus rearranges itself in this way, from a less stable to a more stable structure, it releases some of its binding energy. All that we need to do is to offer the nucleus the chance, as it were, to rearrange itself; the energy will then fly out of itself. To offer it this chance we deliberately make the nucleus unstable by striking and invading it with an extra proton or neutron. If a proton is used, it has to be fired with great energy itself, because the positive nucleus repels its approach. The ideal tool to split the atom is the neutron, for it has no electrical force to overcome on its way to the nucleus.

When a neutron strikes a heavy nucleus it may invade it and make it unstable. The nucleus then breaks up to a more stable form. A nucleus which so rearranges itself from a less to a more stable structure releases some of its binding energy of itself.

Oddly, the rearrangement of the nucleus can be weighed: the parts now weigh less than the whole nucleus did before. The loss of mass exactly balances the energy which has been released—as Einstein foretold some 60 years ago.

Fission is the breaking apart of atoms. It is brought about, as we have just seen, by striking a heavy nucleus with a neutron which invades it and makes it unstable.

But so long as we have to fire neutrons one by one, and break up atoms one by one, we can only get energy in penny packets. To make the breaking or fission of atoms worthwhile, we need a reaction which fires off neutrons of itself as it goes along. Such a reaction was discovered late in the 1930's in the breakup of the explosive variant of uranium.

When this nucleus is struck by a neutron the nucleus breaks up in such a way that, in addition to two roughly equal halves, it also fires off several of its own neutrons. These fly through the rest of the material, and if the piece is large enough each neutron is certain to strike another nucleus and thus set off another burst of energy— and fire off still other neutrons to carry on the reaction.

Therefore, the fission of heavy atoms gives a large return of energy only if it carries itself on from atom to atom in a continuous chain. To do this, each nucleus which breaks up must itself fire off several of its own neutrons. The atoms which do this most violently are the explosive variant of uranium, which was used in the Hiroshima bomb, and man-made plutonium, which was used in the Nagasaki bomb.

A heavy nucleus which breaks up releases some of its binding energy because each of its halves is a more stable nucleus. The middling atoms are, in fact, more stable than the heavy atoms; and they are also more stable than the light atoms.

It is therefore possible to rearrange several light atoms so that they form a more stable nucleus, and to gain energy in this way.

It is also possible to gain energy by taking several very light atoms and rearranging them to make a single nucleus. Here again we are going toward a *more* stable structure and some of the binding energy is therefore released for us.

This process is the building up, or fusion, of atoms. It needs enormous heat, but the return which it gives in energy is also enormous. This is the process which keeps the sun and all the stars aglow. There, at temperatures as high as 20 million degrees Centigrade, atoms of hydrogen are transformed step by step into atoms of helium. The word "helium," in fact, was coined from the Greek name for the sun, because helium was detected in the sun before it was ever found on earth.

The arithmetic of the creation of helium is most revealing. The nucleus of a helium atom has two protons and two neutrons. The following table tells the story of what happens when a nucleus of helium is actually constructed out of these protons and neutrons:

	Weight*
2 neutrons =	2.01788
2 protons =	2.01516
Total =	4.03304
Helium =	4.00280
Difference =	0.03024

*Atomic weights are based on relation to oxygen at '16.

Thus, **paradoxically,**[7] the whole of the helium nucleus is less than the sum of its parts! What happened to the missing mass? The answer is that this "lost" mass has

---

[7] **paradoxically**—seemingly contradictory but nonetheless true.

taken another form: it had been converted into energy. The energy released exactly balances the mass which has been lost—again as Einstein set out in his equation.

We cannot, however, simply assemble helium from protons or neutrons. But, like the sun, we do have a raw material which can be made to fuse into helium. This raw material is made up of special kinds of hydrogen-deuterium (heavy hydrogen) and tritium (extra-heavy hydrogen). In fact, we have available hydrogen atoms in a more concentrated form than the sun has.

But we are at a disadvantage when it comes to making these atoms **fuse**.[8] For they have to be pressed fantastically close together. The difficulty is this: every nucleus is electrically positive. It therefore repels any other nucleus which comes near it. The only way fusion can overcome this repulsion is if every nucleus is moving tremendously fast—that is, if the whole substance is enormously hot so that every part of it is darting about furiously.

Until 20 years ago we could not conceive of producing high enough temperatures on earth to make fusion work. But the atomic bomb gave us a temperature of 150 million degrees Centigrade—though only for perhaps a millionth of a second. It is enough to produce fusion and thus act as a detonator for the H-bomb.[9]

Fusion happens to give rather more energy from each pound of the material than fission can. But there is a graver reason to fear the fusion bomb.

Hydrogen bombs can be made not in pound sizes but perhaps in tons. In a fission bomb the pieces of explosive uranium or plutonium must be kept smaller than a critical size of a few pounds, for a larger piece would explode of itself. But no amount of hydrogen will fuse by itself at our temperatures—it must have the fission

---

[8] **fuse**—to bond together.

[9] H-bomb—hydrogen bomb.

bomb as its trigger. There is therefore no natural limit to the size of a hydrogen bomb.

We think of fusion as a destructive power. A ton of hydrogen detonated over a great city might kill a hundred times as many people as died at Nagasaki. Yet we see that nature has not worked so clumsily. She has used fusion to build all her hundred elements, and from them in turn she has assembled the rich architecture of the living earth. A simple remark about the weights of hydrogen and uranium has opened to us a deep insight into her logic, in which the weight of the atom is a measure of its binding energy and its structure and, we now see, of its very evolution.

We must not despair of fusion because so far we know only how to make it do mischief. Our greatest power over nature rests in understanding her processes; and even Eniwetok[10] can be a step in understanding if we are willing to open our minds to it. The future of man's command of energy will lie in fusion, for this is nature's deepest source. If we can tap this source, the hydrogen in a pint of water will yield more energy than a thousand tons of coal. We are making only a frightened beginning. It is our business, everyone of us as citizens as well as scientists, to put this beginning to its right use: to turn it from destruction and thereby to learn the creative art of nature itself.

---

[10] Eniwetok—island in the Pacific where the first thermonuclear device was tested on November 1, 1951.

QUESTIONS TO CONSIDER

1. How is the ancient Greek idea of the atom different from what we today refer to as an atom?

2. Why are uranium (used in the Hiroshima bomb) and plutonium (used in the Nagasaki bomb) ideal elements for creating a nuclear chain reaction?

3. Why does Bronowski say that the Hydrogen bomb (a fusion device) is so dangerous?

Creator of the Bomb: J. Robert Oppenheimer

When the physicist Enrico Fermi created a self-sustaining uranium chain reaction in 1942, the threat of the bomb became real. A massive industrial and scientific effort to build an atomic weapon, known as the Manhattan Project, was put into place. The highly regarded physicist J. Robert Oppenheimer (1904–1967) was appointed to head the scientific research at a complex near Los Alamos, New Mexico. Oppenheimer recruited a group of world-class physicists and mathematicians and set to work. The work at Los Alamos paid off on July 15, 1945, when the first atomic bomb was exploded at the Trinity site near Los Alamos. The testimonies of his colleagues and his own words speak to Oppenheimer's qualities and his feelings about the atomic bomb.

I. I. Rabi

Oppenheimer understood the whole structure of physics with extraordinary clarity, and not only the structure, but the interactions between the different elements. Hardly any branch of physics was foreign to him. As well as theoretical physics, he also had a vast knowledge of experimental results and methods at his fingertips and would continually amaze experimenters by his great knowledge of their own subject—in some respects exceeding their own, especially in fields of great current interest. It is therefore not surprising that he became an almost mythical figure, especially to experimenters. He could display his great knowledge in their own fields but then could take off into the blue of abstract theory where they could not follow, or only with great difficulty.

Robert Serber

Oppie's way of working with his research students was also original. His group would consist of eight or ten graduate students and about a half dozen postdoctoral fellows. He would meet the group once a day in his office. A little before the appointed time its members would straggle in and dispose themselves on the tables and about the walls. Oppie would come in and discuss with one after another the status of the student's research problem, while the others listened and offered comments. All were exposed to a broad range of topics. Oppenheimer was interested in everything, and one subject after another was introduced and coexisted with all the others. In an afternoon we might discuss electrodynamics, cosmic rays, astrophysics and nuclear physics.

Oppie's relations with his students were not confined to office and classroom. He was a bachelor then, and a part of his social life was intertwined with ours. Often we worked late and continued the discussion through dinner and then later at his apartment on Shasta Road.

When we tired of our problems, or cleaned up the point at issue, the talk would turn to art, music, literature, and politics. If the work was going badly we might give up and go to a movie. Sometimes we took a night off and had a Mexican dinner in Oakland or went to a good restaurant in San Francisco. In the early days this meant taking the Berkeley ferry and a ride across the bay. The ferries back to Berkeley didn't run very often late at night, and this required passing the time waiting for them at the bars and night clubs near the ferry dock. Frequently we missed several ferries.

Glenn Seaborg

I had one difficulty with Oppie that I imagine was common to all who sought his advice, that is, facing his tendency to answer your question even before you had fully stated it. In this respect, I recall taking great pains in formulating my questions to him in such a way that I could put the main thrust of my thoughts as early as possible into every sentence.

Abraham Pais

Any single one of the following contributions would have marked Oppenheimer out as a pre-eminent scientist: his own research work in physics; his influence as a teacher; his leadership at Los Alamos; the growth of the Institute for Advanced Study as a leading center of theoretical physics under his directorship; and his efforts to promote a more common understanding of science. When all is combined, we honor Oppenheimer as a great leader of science. When all is interwoven with the dramatic events that centered around him, we remember Oppenheimer as one of the most remarkable personalities of this century. In the years to come the physicist will speak of him. So will the historian and the psychologist, the playwright and the poet. But it would take the singular combination of talents of this extraordinary man himself to characterize his life in brief. Perhaps Robert has done just that. I shall conclude with a few lines which he wrote many years ago.

"The wealth and variety of physics itself, the greater wealth of the natural sciences taken as a whole, the more familiar, yet still strange and far wider wealth of the life of the human spirit, enriched by complementary, not at once **compatible**[1] ways, **irreducible**[2] one to the other, have a greater harmony. They are the elements of man's sorrow and his splendour, his frailty and his power, his death and his passing, and his undying deeds."

Victor F. Weisskopf

He did not direct from the head office. He was intellectually and even physically present at each significant step; he was present in the laboratory or in the seminar rooms when a new effect was measured, when a new idea was conceived. It was not that he contributed so many ideas or suggestions; he did so sometimes, but his main influence came from his continuous and intense presence, which produced a sense of direct participation in all of us. It created that unique atmosphere of enthusiasm and challenge that pervaded the place throughout its time. I remember vividly the sessions of the co-ordinating council, a regular meeting of all group leaders where progress and failures were reviewed and future plans were discussed. The discussions covered everything: physics, technology, organization, administration, secrecy **regulations**[3] and our relations to the Army.

It was most impressive to see Oppie handle that mixture of international scientific prima donnas, engineers, and army officers, forging them into an enthusiastically

---

[1] **compatible**—a good, workable, or agreeable combination.

[2] **irreducible**—not able to be reduced or made smaller.

[3] **regulations**—principles, rules, or laws.

productive crowd. The project was not without tensions and clashes between personalities, but he dealt with these problems with a light hand, and he knew how to exploit conflicts in a productive way. I remember the weekly **colloquium**,[4] where everyone with a white badge—the mark of an academic degree—participated and listened to talks about all essential aspects of the work. Oppenheimer insisted on having these regular colloquia against the opposition of the security-minded people, who wanted each man only to know his part of the work. He knew that each one must know the whole thing if he was to be creative.

Hans Bethe

He knew and understood everything that went on in the laboratory . . . whether it was chemistry or theoretical physics or machine shop. He could keep it all in his head and coordinate it. It was clear also at Los Alamos that he was intellectually superior to us.

He understood immediately when he heard anything, and fitted it into the general scheme of things and drew the right conclusions. There was just nobody else in that laboratory who came even close to him. In his knowledge. There was human warmth as well. Everybody certainly had the impression that Oppenheimer cared what each particular person was doing. In talking to someone he made it clear that that person's work was important for the success of the whole project. I don't remember any occasion at Los Alamos in which he was nasty to any person, whereas before and after the war he was often that way. At Los Alamos he didn't make anybody feel inferior, not anybody.

---

[4] **colloquium**—an informed meeting to exchange views.

Oppenheimer, on the Trinity Test

We waited until the blast had passed, walked out of the shelter and then it was extremely **solemn.**[5] We knew the world would not be the same. A few people laughed, a few people cried. Most people were silent. I remembered the line from the Hindu scripture, the *Bhagavad-Gita*: Vishnu[6] is trying to persuade the Prince that he should do his duty and to impress him he takes on his multi-armed form and says, "Now I am become Death, the destroyer of worlds." I suppose we all thought that, one way or another.

Oppenheimer, in his speech to the Association of Los Alamos Scientists

One always has to worry that what people say of their motives is not adequate. Many people said different things, and most of them, I think, had some validity. There was in the first place the great concern that our enemy might develop these weapons before we did, and the feeling—at least, in the early days, the very strong feeling—that without atomic weapons it might be very difficult, it might be an impossible, it might be an incredibly long thing to win the war. These things wore off a little as it became clear that the war would be won in any case. Some people, I think, were motivated by curiosity, and rightly so; and some by a sense of adventure, and rightly so. Others had more political arguments and said, "Well, we know that atomic weapons are in principle possible, and it is not right that the threat of their unrealized possibility should hang over the world. It is right that the world should know what can be done in their field and deal with it." And the people added to that that it was a time when all over the world men would be particularly ripe and open for dealing with this problem because of the immediacy of

---

[5] **solemn**—deeply earnest and serious; somber.
[6] Vishnu—one of the principal gods in Hinduism.

the evils of war, because of the universal cry from everyone that one could not go through this thing again, even a war without atomic bombs. And there was finally, and I think rightly, the feeling that there was probably no place in the world where the development of atomic weapons would have a better chance of leading to a reasonable solution, and a smaller chance of leading to disaster, than within the United States. I believe all these things that people said are true, and I think I said them all myself at one time or another.

But when you come right down to it the reason that we did this job is because it was an organic necessity. If you are a scientist you cannot stop such a thing. If you are a scientist you believe that it is good to find out how the world works; that it is good to find out what the realities are; that it is good to turn over to mankind at large the greatest possible power to control the world and to deal with it according to its lights and its values.

QUESTIONS TO CONSIDER

1. How would you describe Robert Oppenheimer?

2. What seems to be the main impression of Oppenheimer from his colleagues?

3. Why do you think Oppenheimer helped to build the atomic bomb?

Decision to
Use the Bomb

Truman's Diary at Potsdam

Harry Truman became President of the United States when Franklin Roosevelt died unexpectedly in April 1945. At the time he took office, Truman knew nothing of the atomic bomb project at Los Alamos. But he was faced quickly with the choice of whether to use the new weapon against Japan. In July, Truman went to Potsdam to meet with the British prime minister Winston Churchill and the Soviet premier Joseph Stalin to discuss postwar Europe and the continuing war against Japan. In his diary, Truman refers to the atomic bomb and the troubles between the allies.

[Potsdam] July 25, 1945

We met at 11 A.M. today. That is Stalin, Churchill and the U.S. President. But I had a most important session with Lord Mountbatten[1] & General Marshall[2] before that. We have discovered the most terrible bomb in the

---

[1] Louis Mountbatten, a British naval officer, was Allied commander in Southeast Asia from 1943 to 1946.

[2] George Marshall was the chief of staff of the United States Army and later served as Secretary of State.

history of the world. It may be the fire destruction prophesied in the Euphrates Valley Era, after Noah and his fabulous Ark.

Anyway we "think" we have found the way to cause a disintegration of the atom. An experiment in the New Mexican desert was startling—to put it mildly. Thirteen pounds of the explosive caused the complete disintegration of a steel tower 60 feet high, created a crater 6 feet deep and 1,200 feet in diameter, knocked over a steel tower 1/2 mile away and knocked men down 10,000 yards away. The explosion was visible for more than 200 miles and audible for 40 miles and more.

This weapon is to be used against Japan between now and August 10th. I have told the Sec. of War, Mr. Stimson, to use it so that military objectives and soldiers and sailors are the target and not women and children. . . . we as the leader of the world for the common welfare cannot drop this terrible bomb on the old capital or the new.

He & I are in accord. The target will be a purely military one and we will issue a warning statement asking the Japs[3] to surrender and save lives. I'm sure they will not do that, but we will have given them the chance. It is certainly a good thing for the world that Hitler's crowd or Stalin's did not discover this atomic bomb. It seems to be the most terrible thing ever discovered, but it can be made the most useful.

At 10:15 I had Gen. Marshall come in and discuss with me the tactical and political situation. He is a level-headed man—so is Mountbatten.

At the Conference Poland and the Bolsheviki land grab came up. Russia helped herself to a slice of Poland and gave Poland a nice slice of Germany, taking also a good slice of East Prussia for herself. Poland has moved in up to the Oder and the west Neisse, taking Stettin and

---

[3] Japs—slang term, often derogatory, that was commonly used during the war to refer to the Japanese.

Silesia as a fact accomplished. My position is that, according to commitments made at Yalta by my predecessor, Germany was to be divided into four occupation zones, one each for Britain, Russia and France and the U.S. If Russia chooses to allow Poland to occupy a part of her zone I am agreeable but title to territory cannot and will not be settled here. For the fourth time I restated my position and explained that territorial cessions had to be made by treaty and ratified by the Senate.

We discussed reparations and movement of populations from East Germany, Czechoslovakia, Austria, Italy and elsewhere. Churchill said Maisky had so defined war booty as to include the German fleet and Merchant Marine. It was a bomb shell and sort of paralyzed the Russkies,[4] but it has a lot of merit.

---

[4] Russkies—a slang term for the Russians.

QUESTIONS TO CONSIDER

1. How would you describe Truman's feelings toward the Japanese?

2. How would you describe his feelings toward Russia?

3. What does Truman seem most concerned about—the war in the Pacific or Russian aggressiveness?

President Truman's Statement about the Bombing of Hiroshima

On August 6, the United States dropped the first atomic bomb on Hiroshima. Early the next day, President Truman released a statement describing the weapon to the public. The President praised the great effort undertaken by the scientists who built the bomb.

THE WHITE HOUSE
Washington, D.C.

IMMEDIATE RELEASE

STATEMENT BY THE PRESIDENT
OF THE UNITED STATES

Sixteen hours ago an American airplane dropped one bomb on Hiroshima and destroyed its usefulness to the enemy. That bomb had more power than 20,000 tons of T.N.T. It had more than two thousand times the blast power of the British "Grand Slam" which is the largest bomb ever yet used in the history of warfare.

The Japanese began the war from the air at Pearl Harbor. They have been repaid many fold. And the end is not yet. With this bomb we have now added a new and revolutionary increase in destruction to supplement the growing power of our armed forces. In their present form these bombs are now in production and even more powerful forms are in development.

It is an atomic bomb. It is a harnessing of the basic power of the universe. The force from which the sun draws its power has been loosed against those who brought war to the Far East.

Before 1939, it was the accepted belief of scientists that it was theoretically possible to release atomic energy. But no one knew any practical method of doing it. By 1942, however, we knew that the Germans were working feverishly to find a way to add atomic energy to the other engines of war with which they hoped to enslave the world. But they failed. We may be grateful to Providence that the Germans got the V-1's and V-2's late and in limited quantities and even more grateful that they did not get the atomic bomb at all.

The battle of the laboratories held fateful risks for us as well as the battles of the air, land and sea, and we have now won the battle of the laboratories as we have won the other battles.

Beginning in 1940, before Pearl Harbor, scientific knowledge useful in war was pooled between the United States and Great Britain, and many priceless helps to our victories have come from that arrangement. Under that general policy the research on the atomic bomb was begun. With American and British scientists working together we entered the race of discovery against the Germans.

The United States had available the large number of scientists of distinction in the many needed areas of knowledge. It had the tremendous industrial and financial resources necessary for the project and they could be devoted to it without undue impairment of other vital war work. In the United States the laboratory work and the production plants, on which a substantial start had already been made, would be out of reach of enemy bombing, while at that time Britain was exposed to constant air attack and was still threatened with the possibility of invasion. For these reasons Prime Minister Churchill and President Roosevelt agreed that it was wise to carry on the project here. We now have two great plants and many lesser works devoted to the production of atomic power. Employment during peak construction numbered 125,000 and over 65,000 individuals are even now engaged in operating the plants. Many have worked there for two and a half years. Few know what they have been producing. They see great quantities of material going in and they see nothing coming out of these plants, for the physical size of the explosive charge is exceedingly small. We have spent two billion dollars on the greatest scientific gamble in history—and won.

But the greatest marvel is not the size of the enterprise, its secrecy, nor its cost, but the achievement of scientific brains in putting together infinitely complex pieces of knowledge held by many men in different fields of science into a workable plan. And hardly less marvellous has been the capacity of industry to design, and of labor to operate, the machines and methods to do things never done before so that the brain child of many minds came forth in physical shape and performed as it was supposed to do. Both science and industry worked under the direction of the United States Army, which achieved a unique success in managing so diverse a problem in the advancement of knowledge in an amazingly short time. It is doubtful if such another combination could be got together in the world. What has been done is the greatest achievement of organized science in history. It was done under high pressure and without failure.

We are now prepared to obliterate more rapidly and completely every productive enterprise the Japanese have above ground in any city. We shall destroy their docks, their factories, and their communications. Let there be no mistake; we shall completely destroy Japan's power to make war.

It was to spare the Japanese people from utter destruction that the ultimatum of July 26[1] was issued at Potsdam. Their leaders promptly rejected that ultimatum. If they do not now accept our terms they may expect a rain of ruin from the air, the like of which has never been seen on this earth. Behind this air attack will follow sea and land forces in such numbers and power as they have not yet seen and with the fighting skill of which they are already well aware.

The Secretary of War, who has kept in personal touch with all phases of the project, will immediately make public a statement giving further details.

His statement will give facts concerning the sites at Oak Ridge near Knoxville, Tennessee, and at Richland near Pasco, Washington, and an installation near Santa Fe, New Mexico. Although the workers at the sites have been making materials to be used in producing the greatest destructive force in history they have not themselves been in danger beyond that of many other occupations, for the utmost care has been taken of their safety.

The fact that we can release atomic energy ushers in a new era in man's understanding of nature's forces. Atomic energy may in the future supplement the power that now comes from coal, oil, and falling water, but at

---

[1] ultimatum of July 26—This declaration, issued by the U.S., England, and China, called for Japan's unconditional surrender.

present it cannot be produced on a basis to compete with them commercially. Before that comes there must be a long period of intensive research.

It has never been the habit of the scientists of this country or the policy of this Government to withhold from the world scientific knowledge. Normally, therefore, everything about the work with atomic energy would be made public.

But under present circumstances it is not intended to divulge the technical processes of production or all the military applications, pending further examination of possible methods of protecting us and the rest of the world from the danger of sudden destruction.

I shall recommend that the Congress of the United States consider promptly the establishment of an appropriate commission to control the production and use of atomic power within the United States. I shall give further consideration and make further recommendations to the Congress as to how atomic power can become a powerful and forceful influence towards the maintenance of world peace.

QUESTIONS TO CONSIDER

1. What does Truman say is the "greatest marvel" of the atomic bomb project?

2. In your opinion, was the atomic bomb one of science's "greatest achievements"? Why or why not?

3. How does Truman envision the future of the atomic bomb?

The Decision to Use the Atomic Bomb

BY HENRY L. STIMSON

Henry L. Stimson was secretary of war under both Presidents Roosevelt and Truman. Stimson was a member of the small committee that advised the President on the study of nuclear fission and was also responsible for overseeing the project to construct the first atomic weapon. Throughout 1945, Stimson was one of the key figures in the discussion of how and when to use the atomic bomb against Japan. When the debate about the use of the bomb developed after the war, Stimson decided to write an account of how the decision was arrived at. His account was published in Harper's *magazine in 1947.*

The policy adopted and steadily pursued by President Roosevelt and his advisers was a simple one. It was to spare no effort in securing the earliest possible successful development of an atomic weapon. The reasons for this policy were equally simple. The original experimental achievement of atomic fission had occurred in Germany in 1938, and it was known that the Germans had continued their experiments. In 1941 and 1942 they were believed to be ahead of us, and it was vital that they should not be the first to bring atomic weapons into the field of battle. Furthermore, if we should be the first to develop the weapon, we should have a great new instrument for shortening the war and minimizing destruction. At no time, from 1941 to 1945, did I ever hear it suggested by the President, or by any other responsible member of the government, that atomic energy should not be used in the war. All of us of course understood the terrible responsibility involved in our attempt to unlock the doors to such a devastating weapon; President Roosevelt particularly spoke to me many times of his own awareness of the **catastrophic**[1] potentialities of our work. But we were at war, and the work must be done. I therefore emphasize that it was our common objective, throughout the war, to be the first to produce an atomic weapon and use it. The possible atomic weapon was considered to be a new and tremendously powerful explosive, as legitimate as any other of the deadly explosive weapons of modern war. The entire purpose was the production of a military weapon; on no other ground could the wartime expenditure of so much time and money have been justified. The exact circumstances in which that weapon might be used were unknown to any of us until the middle of 1945, and when that time came, as we shall presently see, the military use of atomic energy was connected with larger questions of national policy.

U.S. Policy toward Japan in July 1945

The principal political, social, and military objective of the United States in the summer of 1945 was the prompt and complete surrender of Japan. Only the

---

[1] **catastrophic**—terrible, tragic, ruinous.

complete destruction of her military power could open the way to lasting peace.

Japan, in July 1945, had been seriously weakened by our increasingly violent attacks. It was known to us that she had gone so far as to make tentative proposals to the Soviet government, hoping to use the Russians as **mediators**[2] in a negotiated peace. These vague proposals contemplated the retention by Japan of important conquered areas and were therefore not considered seriously. There was as yet no indication of any weakening in the Japanese determination to fight rather than accept unconditional surrender. If she should persist in her fight to the end, she had still a great military force.

In the middle of July 1945, the intelligence section of the War Department General Staff estimated Japanese military strength as follows: in the home islands, slightly under 2,000,000; in Korea, Manchuria, China proper, and Formosa, slightly over 2,000,000; in French Indo-China, Thailand, and Burma, over 200,000; in the East Indies area, including the Philippines, over 500,000; in the by-passed Pacific islands, over 100,000. The total strength of the Japanese Army was estimated at about 5,000,000 men. These estimates later proved to be in very close agreement with official Japanese figures.

The Japanese Army was in much better condition than the Japanese Navy and Air Force. The Navy had practically ceased to exist except as a harrying force against an invasion fleet. The Air Force had been reduced mainly to reliance upon Kamikaze, or suicide, attacks. These latter, however, had already inflicted serious damage on our seagoing forces, and their possible effectiveness in a last ditch fight was a matter of real concern to our naval leaders.

As we understood it in July, there was a very strong possibility that the Japanese government might determine

---

[2] **mediators**—persons who work with opposing or conflicting parties and attempt to help them reach an acceptable compromise.

upon resistance to the end, in all the areas of the Far East under its control. In such an event the Allies would be faced with the enormous task of destroying an armed force of five million men and five thousand suicide aircraft, belonging to a race which had already amply demonstrated its ability to fight literally to the death.

The strategic plans of our armed forces for the defeat of Japan, as they stood in July, had been prepared without reliance upon the atomic bomb, which had not yet been tested in New Mexico. We were planning an intensified sea and air blockade, and greatly intensified strategic air bombing, through the summer and early fall, to be followed on November 1 by an invasion of the southern island of Kyushu. This would be followed in turn by an invasion of the main island of Honshu in the spring of 1946. The total U. S. military and naval force involved in this grand design was of the order of 5,000,000 men; if all those indirectly concerned are included, it was larger still.

We estimated that if we should be forced to carry this plan to its conclusion, the major fighting would not end until the latter part of 1946, at the earliest. I was informed that such operations might be expected to cost over a million casualties, to American forces alone. Additional large losses might be expected among our allies, and, of course, if our campaign were successful and if we could judge by previous experience, enemy casualties would be much larger than our own.

It was already clear in July that even before the invasion we should be able to inflict enormously severe damage on the Japanese homeland by the combined application of "conventional" sea and air power. The critical question was whether this kind of action would **induce**[3] surrender. It therefore became necessary to consider very carefully the probable state of mind of the

---

[3] **induce**—bring about, create.

enemy, and to assess with accuracy the line of conduct which might end his will to resist.

With these considerations in mind, I wrote a memorandum for the President, on July 2, which I believe fairly represents the thinking of the American government as it finally took shape in action. This memorandum was prepared after discussion and general agreement with Joseph C. Grew, Acting Secretary of State, and Secretary of the Navy Forrestal, and when I discussed it with the President, he expressed his general approval.

July 2, 1945. Memorandum for the President.
PROPOSED PROGRAM FOR JAPAN

1. The plans of operation up to and including the first landing have been authorized and the preparations for the operation are now actually going on. This situation was accepted by all members of your conference on Monday, June 18.

2. There is reason to believe that the operation for the occupation of Japan following the landing may be a very long, costly, and arduous struggle on our part. The terrain, much of which I have visited several times, has left the impression on my memory of being one which would be susceptible to a last ditch defense such as has been made on Iwo Jima and Okinawa and which of course is very much larger than either of those two areas. According to my recollection it will be much more unfavorable with regard to tank maneuvering than either the Philippines or Germany.

3. If we once land on one of the main islands and begin a forceful occupation of Japan, we shall probably have cast the die of last ditch resistance. The Japanese are highly patriotic and certainly susceptible to calls for fanatical resistance to repel an invasion. Once started in actual invasion, we shall in my opinion have to go through with an even more bitter finish fight than in Germany. We shall incur the losses incident to such a war and we shall have to leave the Japanese islands even more thoroughly destroyed than was the case with Germany. This would be due both to the difference in the Japanese and German personal character and the differences in the size and character of the terrain through which the operations will take place.

4. A question then comes: Is there any alternative to such a forceful occupation of Japan which will secure for us the equivalent of an unconditional surrender of her forces and a permanent destruction of her power again to strike an aggressive blow at the "peace of the Pacific"? I am inclined to think that there is enough such chance to make it well worthwhile our giving them a warning of what is to come and a definite opportunity to capitulate. As above suggested, it should be tried before the actual forceful occupation of the homeland islands is begun and furthermore the warning should be given in ample time to permit a national reaction to set in.

We have the following enormously favorable factors on our side—factors much weightier than those we had against Germany:

Japan has no allies.

Her navy is nearly destroyed and she is vulnerable to a surface and underwater blockade which can deprive her of sufficient food and supplies for her population.

She is terribly vulnerable to our concentrated air attack upon her crowded cities, industrial and food resources.

She has against her not only the Anglo-American forces but the rising forces of China and the ominous threat of Russia.

We have inexhaustible and untouched industrial resources to bring to bear against her diminishing potential.

We have great moral superiority through being the victim of her first sneak attack.

The problem is to translate these advantages into prompt and economical achievement of our objectives. I believe Japan is susceptible to reason in such a crisis to a much greater extent than is indicated by our current press and other current *comment. Japan is not a nation composed wholly of mad fanatics of an entirely different mentality from ours. On the contrary, she has within the past century shown herself to possess extremely intelligent people, capable in an unprecedentedly short time of adopting not only the complicated technique of **Occidental**[4] civilization but to a substantial extent their culture and their political and social ideas. Her advance in all these respects during the short period of sixty or seventy years has been one of the most astounding feats of national progress in history—a leap from the isolated **feudalism**[5] of centuries into the position of one of the six or seven great powers of the world. She has not only built up powerful armies and navies. She has maintained an honest and effective national finance and respected position in many of the sciences in which we pride ourselves. Prior to the forcible seizure of power over her government by the fanatical military group in 1931, she had for ten years lived a reasonably responsible and respectable international life.*

My own opinion is in her favor on the two points involved in this question:

a. I think the Japanese nation has the mental intelligence and versatile capacity in such a crisis to recognize the folly of a fight to the finish and to accept the proffer of what will amount to an unconditional surrender; and

b. I think she has within her population enough liberal leaders (although now submerged by the terrorists) to be depended upon for her reconstruction as a responsible member of the family of nations. I think she is better in this last respect than Germany was. Her liberals yielded only at the point of the pistol and, so far as I am aware, their liberal attitude has not been personally subverted in the way which was so general in Germany.

---

[4] **Occidental**—characteristic of countries of Europe and the Western Hemisphere.

[5] **feudalism**—a political system found in Europe in which farmers worked the land for their lord, whom they paid in crops and to whom they gave their complete loyalty.

On the other hand, I think that the attempt to exterminate her armies and her population by gunfire or other means will tend to produce a fusion of race solidity and antipathy which has no analogy in the case of Germany. We have a national interest in creating, if possible, a condition wherein the Japanese nation may live as a peaceful and useful member of the future Pacific community.

5. It is therefore my conclusion that a carefully timed warning be given to Japan by the chief representatives of the United States, Great Britain, China, and, if then a belligerent, Russia by calling upon Japan to surrender, and permit the occupation of her country in order to insure its complete demilitarization for the sake of the future peace.

This warning should contain the following elements:

The varied and overwhelming character of the force we are about to bring to bear on the islands.

The inevitability and completeness of the destruction which the full application of this force will entail.

The determination of the Allies to destroy permanently all authority and influence of those who have deceived and misled the country into embarking on world conquest.

The determination of the Allies to limit Japanese sovereignty to her main islands and to render them powerless to mount and support another war.

*The disavowal of any attempt to **extirpate**[6] the Japanese as a race or to destroy them as a nation.*

*A statement of our readiness, once her economy is purged of its **militaristic**[7] influence, to permit the Japanese to maintain such industries, particularly of a light consumer character, as offer no threat of aggression against their neighbors, but which can produce a sustaining economy, and provide a reasonable standard of living. The statement should indicate our willingness, for this purpose, to give Japan trade access to external raw materials, but no longer any control over the*

---

[6] **extirpate**—destroy completely, wipe out.

[7] **militaristic**—relating to soldiers and the military.

sources of supply outside her main islands. It should also indicate our willingness, in accordance with our now established foreign trade policy, in due course to enter into mutually advantageous trade relations with her.

The withdrawal from their country as soon as the above objectives of the Allies are accomplished, and as soon as there has been established a peacefully inclined government, of a character representative of the masses of the Japanese people. I personally think that if in saying this we should add that we do not exclude a constitutional monarchy under her present **dynasty**,[8] it would substantially add to the chances of acceptance.

6. Success of course will depend on the potency of the warning which we give her. She has an extremely sensitive national pride and, as we are now seeing every day, when actually locked with the enemy will fight to the very death. For that reason the warning must be tendered before the actual invasion has occurred and while the impending destruction, though clear beyond peradventure, has not yet reduced her to **fanatical**[9] despair. If Russia is a part of the threat, the Russian attack, if actual, must not have progressed too far. Our own bombing should be confined to military objectives as far as possible.

It is important to emphasize the double character of the suggested warning. It was designed to promise destruction if Japan resisted, and hope, if she surrendered.

It will be noted that the atomic bomb is not mentioned in this memorandum. On grounds of secrecy the bomb was never mentioned except when absolutely necessary, and furthermore, it had not yet been tested. It was of course well forward in our minds, as the memorandum was written and discussed, that the bomb would be the best possible sanction if our warning were rejected.

---

[8] **dynasty**—a series of rulers from the same family or line.

[9] **fanatical**—marked by extreme zeal or desire.

The Use of the Bomb

The adoption of the policy outlined in the memorandum of July 2 was a decision of high politics; once it was accepted by the President, the position of the atomic bomb in our planning became quite clear. I find that I stated in my diary, as early as June 19, that "the last chance warning . . . must be given before an actual landing of the ground forces in Japan, and fortunately the plans provide for enough time to bring in the sanctions to our warning in the shape of heavy ordinary bombing attack and an attack of S-1." S-1 was a code name for the atomic bomb.

There was much discussion in Washington about the timing of the warning to Japan. The controlling factor in the end was the date already set for the Potsdam meeting of the Big Three. It was President Truman's decision that such a warning should be solemnly issued by the U.S. and the U.K. from this meeting, with the concurrence of the head of the Chinese government, so that it would be plain that *all* of Japan's principal enemies were in entire unity. This was done, in the Potsdam ultimatum of July 26, which very closely followed the above memorandum of July 2, with the exception that it made no mention of the Japanese Emperor.

On July 28 the Premier of Japan, Suzuki, rejected the Potsdam **ultimatum**[10] by announcing that it was "unworthy of public notice." In the face of this rejection we could only proceed to demonstrate that the ultimatum had meant exactly what it said when it stated that if the Japanese continued the war, "the full application of our military power, backed by our resolve, will mean the inevitable and complete destruction of the Japanese armed forces and just as inevitably the utter devastation of the Japanese homeland."

---

[10] **ultimatum**—a final offer made by one party to another.

For such a purpose the atomic bomb was an eminently suitable weapon. The New Mexico test occurred while we were at Potsdam, on July 16. It was immediately clear that the power of the bomb measured up to our highest estimates. We had developed a weapon of such a revolutionary character that its use against the enemy might well be expected to produce exactly the kind of shock on the Japanese ruling oligarchy which we desired, strengthening the position of those who wished peace, and weakening that of the military party.

Because of the importance of the atomic mission against Japan, the detailed plans were brought to me by the military staff for approval. With President Truman's warm support I struck off the list of suggested targets the city of Kyoto. Although it was a target of considerable military importance, it had been the ancient capital of Japan and was a shrine of Japanese art and culture. We determined that it should be spared. I approved four other targets including the cities of Hiroshima and Nagasaki.

Hiroshima was bombed on August 6, and Nagasaki on August 9. These two cities were active working parts of the Japanese war effort. One was an army center; the other was naval and industrial. Hiroshima was the headquarters of the Japanese Army defending southern Japan and was a major military storage and assembly point. Nagasaki was a major seaport and it contained several large industrial plants of great wartime importance. We believed that our attacks had struck cities which must certainly be important to the Japanese military leaders, both Army and Navy, and we waited for a result. We waited one day.

Many accounts have been written about the Japanese surrender. After a prolonged Japanese cabinet session in which the deadlock was broken by the Emperor himself, the offer to surrender was made on August 10. It was based on the Potsdam terms, with a reservation concerning the sovereignty of the Emperor. While the Allied reply made no promises other than those already given, it implicitly recognized the Emperor's position by prescribing that his power must be subject to the orders of the Allied Supreme Commander. These terms were accepted on August 14 by the Japanese, and the instrument of surrender was formally signed on September 2, in Tokyo Bay. Our great objective was thus achieved, and all the evidence I have seen indicates that the controlling factor in the final Japanese decision to accept our terms of surrender was the atomic bomb.

The two atomic bombs which we had dropped were the only ones we had ready, and our rate of production at the time was very small. Had the war continued until the projected invasion on November 1, additional fire raids of B-29's would have been more destructive of life and property than the very limited number of atomic raids which we could have executed in the same period. But the atomic bomb was more than a weapon of terrible destruction; it was a psychological weapon. In March 1945 our Air Force had launched its first great incendiary raid on the Tokyo area. In this raid more damage was done and more casualties were inflicted than was the case at Hiroshima. Hundreds of bombers took part and hundreds of tons of **incendiaries**[11] were dropped. Similar successive raids burned out a great part of the urban area of Japan, but the Japanese fought on. On August 6 one B-29 dropped a single atomic bomb on Hiroshima. Three days later a second bomb was dropped on Nagasaki and the war was over. So far as the Japanese could know, our ability to execute atomic attacks, if necessary by many planes at a time, was unlimited. As Dr. Karl Compton has said, "it was not one atomic bomb, or two, which brought surrender; it was the experience of what an atomic bomb will actually do to a community, *plus the dread of many more,* that was effective."

---

[11] **incendiaries**—bombs, especially ones capable of causing fires.

The bomb thus served exactly the purpose we intended. The peace party was able to take the path of surrender, and the whole weight of the Emperor's prestige was exerted in favor of peace. When the Emperor ordered surrender, and the small but dangerous group of fanatics who opposed him were brought under control, the Japanese became so subdued that the great undertaking of occupation and **disarmament**[12] was completed with unprecedented ease.

A Personal Summary

In the foregoing pages I have tried to give an accurate account of my own personal observations of the circumstances which led up to the use of the atomic bomb and the reasons which underlay our use of it. To me they have always seemed compelling and clear, and I cannot see how any person vested with such responsibilities as mine could have taken any other course or given any other advice to his chiefs.

Two great nations were approaching contact in a fight to a finish which would begin on November 1, 1945. Our enemy, Japan, commanded forces of somewhat over 5,000,000 armed men. Men of these armies had already inflicted upon us, in our breakthrough of the outer perimeter of their defenses, over 300,000 battle casualties. Enemy armies still unbeaten had the strength to cost us a million more. *As long as the Japanese government refused to surrender,* we should be forced to take and hold the ground, and smash the Japanese ground armies, by close-in fighting of the same desperate and costly kind that we had faced in the Pacific islands for nearly four years.

In the light of the formidable problem which thus confronted us, I felt that every possible step should be taken to compel a surrender of the homelands, and a

---

[12] **disarmament**—lay down arms or weapons, surrender.

withdrawal of all Japanese troops from the Asiatic mainland and from other positions, before we had commenced an invasion. We held two cards to assist us in such an effort. One was the traditional **veneration**[13] in which the Japanese Emperor was held by his subjects and the power which was thus vested in him over his loyal troops. It was for this reason that I suggested in my memorandum of July 2 that his dynasty should be continued. The second card was the use of the atomic bomb in the manner best calculated to persuade that Emperor and the counselors about him to submit to our demand for what was essentially unconditional surrender, placing his immense power over his people and his troops subject to our orders.

In order to end the war in the shortest possible time and to avoid the enormous losses of human life which otherwise confronted us, I felt that we must use the Emperor as our instrument to command and compel his people to cease fighting and subject themselves to our authority through him, and that to accomplish this we must give him and his controlling advisers a compelling reason to accede to our demands. This reason furthermore must be of such a nature that his people could understand his decision. The bomb seemed to me to furnish a unique instrument for that purpose.

My chief purpose was to end the war in victory with the least possible cost in the lives of the men in the armies which I had helped to raise. In the light of the alternatives which, on a fair estimate, were open to us I believe that no man, in our position and subject to our responsibilities, holding in his hands a weapon of such possibilities for accomplishing this purpose and saving those lives, could have failed to use it and afterwards looked his countrymen in the face.

---

[13] **veneration**—profound respect.

As I read over what I have written, I am aware that much of it, in this year of peace, may have a harsh and unfeeling sound. It would perhaps be possible to say the same things and say them more gently. But I do not think it would be wise. As I look back over the five years of my service as Secretary of War, I see too many stern and heartrending decisions to be willing to pretend that war is anything else than what it is. The face of war is the face of death; death is an inevitable part of every order that a wartime leader gives. The decision to use the atomic bomb was a decision that brought death to over a hundred thousand Japanese. No explanation can change that fact and I do not wish to gloss it over. But this deliberate, **premeditated**[14] destruction was our least abhorrent choice. The destruction of Hiroshima and Nagasaki put an end to the Japanese war. It stopped the fire raids, and the strangling blockade; it ended the ghastly specter of a clash of great land armies.

In this last great action of the Second World War we were given final proof that war is death. War in the twentieth century has grown steadily more barbarous, more destructive, more debased in all its aspects. Now, with the release of atomic energy, man's ability to destroy himself is very nearly complete. The bombs dropped on Hiroshima and Nagasaki ended a war. They also made it wholly clear that we must never have another war. This is the lesson men and leaders everywhere must learn, and I believe that when they learn it they will find a way to lasting peace. There is no other choice.

---

[14] **premeditated**—thought out in advance, planned.

QUESTIONS TO CONSIDER

1. What are a few reasons Stimson gives for the decision to use the atomic bomb? Which was the most important to him?

2. Reread Stimson's description of the warning to Japan (pages 47–48). Does it succeed in its goal to "promise destruction if Japan resisted, and hope if she surrendered"? Support your opinion.

3. Do you think that Stimson's account is impartial and unbiased? On what do you base your answer?

4. In what ways was the atomic bomb a "psychological weapon"?

A Petition to the President of the United States

BY THE ATOMIC SCIENTISTS

On July 17, 1945, a group of the scientists working on the atomic bomb project sent a petition to President Truman asking him not to use the bomb until Japan had had the chance to surrender. The petition had been circulated through the community as scientists became more and more concerned with the potential effects of their creation. The atomic bomb and other nuclear weapons still present a troubling issue for the scientists who have the ability to understand and improve them.

Discoveries of which the people of the United States are not aware may affect the welfare of this nation in the near future. The liberation of atomic power which has been achieved places atomic bombs in the hands of the Army. It places in your hands, as Commander-in-Chief, the fateful decision whether or not to sanction the use of such bombs in the present phase of the war against Japan.

We, the undersigned scientists, have been working in the field of atomic power. Until recently we have had to fear that the United States might be attacked by atomic bombs during this war and that her only defense might lie in a counterattack by the same means. Today, with the defeat of Germany, this danger is averted and we feel impelled to say what follows:

The war has to be brought speedily to a successful conclusion and attacks by atomic bombs may very well be an effective method of warfare. We feel, however, that such attacks on Japan could not be justified, at least not unless the terms which will be imposed after the war on Japan were made public in detail and Japan were given an opportunity to surrender.

If such public announcement gave assurance to the Japanese that they could look to a life devoted to peaceful pursuits in their homeland and if Japan still refused to surrender our nation might then, in certain circumstances, find itself forced to resort to the use of atomic bombs. Such a step, however, ought not to be made at any time without seriously considering the moral responsibilities which are involved.

The development of atomic power will provide the nations with new means of destruction. The atomic bombs at our disposal represent only the first step in this direction, and there is almost no limit to the destructive power which will become available in the course of their future development. Thus a nation which sets the precedent of using these newly liberated forces of nature for purposes of destruction may have to bear the responsibility of opening the door to an era of devastation on an unimaginable scale.

If after this war a situation is allowed to develop in the world which permits rival powers to be in uncontrolled possession of these new means of destruction, the cities of the United States as well as the cities of other nations will be in continuous danger of sudden

annihilation.[1] All the resources of the United States, moral and material, may have to be mobilized to prevent the advent of such a world situation. Its prevention is at present the solemn responsibility of the United States—singled out by virtue of her lead in the field of atomic power.

The added material strength which this lead gives to the United States brings with it the obligation of restraint and if we were to **violate**[2] this obligation our moral position would be weakened in the eyes of the world and in our own eyes. It would then be more difficult for us to live up to our responsibility of bringing the unloosened forces of destruction under control.

In view of the foregoing, we, the undersigned, respectfully petition: first, that you exercise your power as Commander-in-Chief, to rule that the United States shall not resort to the use of atomic bombs in this war unless the terms which will be imposed upon Japan have been made public in detail and Japan knowing these terms has refused to surrender; second, that in such an event the question whether or not to use atomic bombs be decided by you in the light of the considerations presented in this petition as well as all the other moral responsibilities which are involved.

---

[1] **annihilation**—utter destruction.

[2] **violate**—to break or disregard the law.

QUESTIONS TO CONSIDER

1. Do you think the scientists were right about the responsibility of being the first nation to use a nuclear weapon? Why or why not?

2. What did the scientists view as the postwar threat of nuclear weapons? Were they right?

3. How would you describe this petition? Was it naïve? Was it forward-thinking? What details in the petition helped you infer the answer?

Thank God for the Atom Bomb

BY PAUL FUSSELL

The American writer Paul Fussell is a veteran of World War II who, in 1981, wrote an essay describing the veteran's viewpoint on the use of the atomic bomb. Fussell, the author of several highly praised books, describes the world of the soldier, far from ethical concerns and debates on moral obligation: a world of destruction where one's personal fate is all important. Fussell's views are highly representative of the generation that fought in World War II.

Writing on the forty-second anniversary of the atom-bombing of Hiroshima and Nagasaki, I want to consider something suggested by the long debate about the **ethics**,[1] if any, of that ghastly affair. Namely, the importance of experience, sheer, vulgar experience, in influencing, if not determining, one's views about that use of the atom bomb.

---

[1] **ethics**—a set of principles about what is the right conduct.

The experience I'm talking about is having to come to grips, face to face, with an enemy who designs your death. The experience is common to those in the marines and the infantry and even the line navy, to those, in short, who fought the Second World War mindful always that their mission was, as they were repeatedly assured, "to close with the enemy and destroy him." *Destroy*, notice: not hurt, frighten, drive away, or capture. I think there's something to be learned about that war, as well as about the tendency of historical memory unwittingly to resolve **ambiguity**[2] and generally clean up the premises, by considering the way testimonies **emanating**[3] from real war experience tend to complicate attitudes about the most cruel ending of that most cruel war.

"What did you do in the Great War, Daddy?" The recruiting poster deserves ridicule and contempt, of course, but here its question is embarrassingly relevant, and the problem is one that touches on the dirty little secret of social class in America. Arthur T. Hadley said recently that those for whom the use of the A-bomb was "wrong" seem to be implying "that it would have been better to allow thousands on thousands of American and Japanese infantrymen to die in honest hand-to-hand combat on the beaches than to drop those two bombs." People holding such views, he notes, "do not come from the ranks of society that produce infantrymen or pilots." And there's an **eloquence**[4] problem: most of those with firsthand experience of the war at its worst were not elaborately educated people. Relatively inarticulate, most have remained silent about what they know. That is, few of those destined to be blown to pieces if the main Japanese islands had been invaded went on to become our most effective men of letters or impressive ethical theorists or professors of contemporary history or of

---

[2] **ambiguity**—uncertainty or doubtfulness.

[3] **emanating**—coming from.

[4] **eloquence**—phrased or spoken powerfully and persuasively.

international law. The testimony of experience has tended to come from rough diamonds—James Jones is an example—who went through the war as enlisted men in the infantry or the Marine Corps.

Anticipating objections from those without such experience, in his book *WWII* Jones carefully prepares for his chapter on the A-bombs by detailing the plans already in motion for the infantry assaults on the home islands of Kyushu (thirteen divisions scheduled to land in November 1945) and ultimately Honshu (sixteen divisions scheduled for March 1946). Planners of the invasion assumed that it would require a full year, to November 1946, for the Japanese to be sufficiently worn down by land combat attrition to surrender. By that time, one million American casualties was the expected price. Jones observes that the forthcoming invasion of Kyushu "was well into its collecting and stockpiling stages before the war ended." (The island of Saipan was designated a main ammunition and supply base for the invasion, and if you go there today you can see some of the assembled stuff still sitting there.) "The assault troops were chosen and already in training," Jones reminds his readers, and he illuminates by the light of experience what this meant:

> What it must have been like to some old-timer buck sergeant or staff sergeant who had been through Guadalcanal or Bougainville or the Philippines, to stand on some beach and watch this huge war machine beginning to stir and move all around him and know that he very likely had survived this far only to fall dead on the dirt of Japan's home islands, hardly bears thinking about.

Another bright enlisted man, this one an experienced marine destined for the assault on Honshu, adds his testimony. Former Pfc. E. B. Sledge, author of the splendid memoir *With the Old Breed at Peleliu and Okinawa*, noticed at the time that the fighting grew "more vicious the closer we got to Japan," with the carnage of Iwo Jima and Okinawa worse than what had gone before. He points out that

> What we had *experienced* [my emphasis] in fighting the Japs (pardon the expression) on Peleliu and Okinawa caused us to formulate some very definite opinions that the invasion . . . would be a ghastly bloodletting. . . . It would shock the American public and the world. [Every Japanese] soldier, civilian, woman, and child would fight to the death with whatever weapons they had, rifle, grenade, or bamboo **spear**.[5]

The Japanese pre-invasion patriotic song, "One Hundred Million Souls for the Emperor," says Sledge, "meant just that." Universal national kamikaze was the point. One kamikaze pilot, discouraged by his unit's failure to impede the Americans very much despite the bizarre casualties it caused, wrote before diving his plane onto an American ship, "I see the war situation becoming more desperate. All Japanese must become soldiers and die for the Emperor." Sledge's First Marine Division was to land close to the Yokosuka Naval Base, "one of the most heavily defended sectors of the island." The marines were told, he recalls, that

> due to the strong beach defenses, caves, tunnels, and numerous Jap suicide torpedo boats and manned mines, few Marines in the first five assault waves would get ashore alive—my

---

[5] **spear**—a weapon with a long shaft and a sharp point on one end.

company was scheduled to be in the first and second waves. The veterans in the outfit felt we had already run out of luck anyway. . . . We viewed the invasion with complete resignation that we would be killed—either on the beach or inland.

And the invasion was going to take place: there's no question about that. It was not theoretical or merely rumored in order to scare the Japanese. By July 10, 1945, the prelanding naval and **aerial**[6] bombardment of the coast had begun, and the battleships *Iowa*, *Missouri*, *Wisconsin*, and *King George V* were steaming up and down the coast, softening it up with their sixteen-inch shells.

On the other hand, John Kenneth Galbraith is persuaded that the Japanese would have surrendered surely by November without an invasion. He thinks the A-bombs were unnecessary and unjustified because the war was ending anyway. The A-bombs meant, he says, "a difference, at most, of two or three weeks." But at the time, with no indication that surrender was on the way, the kamikazes were sinking American vessels, the *Indianapolis* was sunk (880 men killed), and Allied casualties were running to over 7,000 per week. "Two or three weeks," says Galbraith. Two weeks more means 14,000 more killed and wounded, three weeks more, 21,000. Those weeks mean the world if you're one of those thousands or related to one of them. During the time between the dropping of the Nagasaki bomb on August 9 and the actual surrender on the fifteenth, the war pursued its accustomed course: on the twelfth of August eight captured American fliers were executed (heads chopped off); the fifty-first United States submarine, *Bonefish*, was sunk (all aboard drowned); the destroyer *Callaghan* went down, the seventieth to be

---

[6] **aerial**—from the air.

sunk, and the Destroyer Escort *Underhill* was lost. That's a bit of what happened in six days of the two or three weeks posited by Galbraith. What did he do in the war? He worked in the Office of Price Administration in Washington. . . .

In general, the principle is, the farther from the scene of horror, the easier the talk. One young combat naval officer close to the action wrote home in the fall of 1943, just before the marines underwent the agony of Tarawa: "When I read that we will fight the Japs for years if necessary and will sacrifice hundreds of thousands if we must, I always like to check from where he's talking: it's seldom out here." That was Lieutenant (j.g.) John F. Kennedy. And Winston Churchill, with an irony perhaps too broad and easy, noted in Parliament that the people who preferred invasion to A-bombing seemed to have "no intention of proceeding to the Japanese front themselves. . . ."

On Okinawa, only weeks before Hiroshima, 123,000 Japanese and Americans *killed* each other. (About 140,000 Japanese died at Hiroshima.) "Just awful" was the comment on the Okinawa slaughter not of some pacifist but of General MacArthur. On July 14, 1945, General Marshall sadly informed the Combined Chiefs of Staff—he was not trying to scare the Japanese—that it's "now clear . . . that in order to finish with the Japanese quickly, it will be necessary to invade the industrial heart of Japan." The invasion was definitely on, as I know because I was to be in it.

When the atom bomb ended the war, I was in the Forty-fifth Infantry Division, which had been through the European war so thoroughly that it had needed to be reconstituted two or three times. We were in a staging area near Rheims, ready to be shipped back across the United States for refresher training at Fort Lewis, Washington, and then sent on for final preparation in the Philippines. My division, like most of the ones transferred from Europe, was to take part in the invasion of Honshu. (The earlier landing on Kyushu was to be carried out by the 700,000 infantry already in the Pacific, those with whom James Jones has sympathized.) I was a twenty-one-year-old second lieutenant of infantry leading a rifle platoon. Although still officially fit for combat, in the German war I had already been wounded in the back and the leg badly enough to be adjudged, after the war, 40 percent disabled. But even if my leg buckled and I fell to the ground whenever I jumped out of the back of a truck, and even if the very idea of more combat made me breathe in gasps and shake all over, my condition was held to be adequate for the next act. When the atom bombs were dropped and news began to circulate that "Operation Olympic" would not, after all, be necessary, when we learned to our astonishment that we would not be obliged in a few months to rush up the beaches near Tokyo assault-firing while being machine-gunned, mortared, and shelled, for all the practiced **phlegm**[7] of our tough facades we broke down and cried with relief and joy. We were going to live. We were going to grow to adulthood after all. The killing was all going to be over, and peace was actually going to be the state of things. When the *Enola Gay*[8] dropped its package, "There were cheers," says John Toland, "over the intercom; it meant the end of the war." Down on the ground the reaction of Sledge's marine buddies when they heard the news was more solemn and complicated. They heard about the end of the war

> with quiet disbelief coupled with an indescribable sense of relief. We thought the Japanese would never surrender. Many refused to believe it. . . . Sitting in stunned silence, we remembered our dead. So many dead. So many maimed.

---

[7] **phlegm**—coolness and calm fortitude.

[8] *Enola Gay*—the plane that dropped the atomic bomb on Hiroshima.

So many bright futures consigned to the ashes of the past. So many dreams lost in the madness that had engulfed us. Except for a few widely scattered shouts of joy, the survivors of the abyss sat hollow-eyed and silent, trying to comprehend a world without war.

QUESTIONS TO CONSIDER

1. What is the importance of experience to Fussell?

2. How would you describe the attitude toward war of the soldiers Fussell quotes from in his essay? What did the use of the atomic bomb represent to them?

3. Do you think Fussell is fair to those who think that the use of the bomb was unjustified? Why or why not?

4. What is your opinion about using the atomic bomb after reading Fussell's views?

from

"The Good War": An Oral History of World War Two

BY STUDS TERKEL

Studs Terkel's The Good War *is an oral history of World War II. Terkel spent years interviewing every kind of participant in the war and was able to present first-person accounts of most faces of the conflict. Akira Miuri was a teenager in Japan during the war and describes life on the Japanese home front and his reactions to the atomic bomb and the surrender. John Kenneth Galbraith, a famous economist, worked for the United States government as a civilian during the war. He describes his job to assess the effectiveness of airpower during the war.*

AKIRA MIURI

He is a professor of Japanese language and literature at the University of Wisconsin, Madison.

The day the war broke out, December 8, Tokyo time, I heard the Pearl Harbor news on the radio. Though we had been reading in the paper that this sort of thing might occur, it still came as a shock. I was fourteen, in middle school. My father was an English teacher. Both my parents, two brothers, and four sisters were all living together. We were at first elated by the news of this victory. It overshadowed worries about the war. We weren't thinking about how it would turn out.

My father's feelings were **ambivalent**.[1] He had studied at Oxford for a couple of years and came back to Japan to teach. I suspect he was pro-West secretly, but suppressed these feelings and became quite patriotic.

In '43, students who had enjoyed deferment were beginning to be drafted, especially students who had been in the humanities. The sciences were not touched as much.

My older brother, who was two years older, was drafted. They made him a **reconnaissance**[2] officer. One day his plane crashed. He and the pilot were killed. In '45, just four months before the end of the war. Two of my sisters married just before the war. Both their husbands were drafted. One was killed in Okinawa. There were a lot of casualties among our relatives and friends.

In Japan, we were not drafted until we were twenty. Toward the end of the war, draft age was lowered to nineteen. I was a few months younger than nineteen when it was over, so fortunately I was never drafted.

Even before the war, Japan had been under military rule, so our education didn't change that much. We did

---

[1] **ambivalent**—divided, uncertain or sure.

[2] **reconnaissance**—gathering military information about the enemy or enemy's positions.

spend more time with patriotic material in history classes and were being taught how to march and how to shoot. We took it in stride without much questioning.

In the beginning, the war was still distant to us. We sent off our relatives and friends with cheery smiles and military songs. We didn't see any bombing yet, so we were not really aware of what war was like.

Doolittle's raids began in '42 and '43. When I saw a couple of American planes in the sky, I realized it was coming closer. After Doolittle's first attacks on Tokyo, nothing happened for a time. America started invading all those Pacific islands. When they took Saipan and built a huge airfield there, it really began. We saw these bombers high above Tokyo. They came in droves early in '44.

In '44, all the high schools were closed so the students could work in the factories. Everybody was mobilized for the war effort. My classmates and I were sent to a metal factory, where they were building airplane parts. I was seventeen then.

The younger kids were all evacuated from Tokyo and sent to the countryside. The air raids were now getting worse and quite heavy. I was awakened by air-raid sirens and could see the western sky lighted up by fire bombs. It looked like a big display of fireworks. Fortunately, the residential area where I lived was not hit. We were very lucky, because in Tokyo it was hard to distinguish factory areas from dwelling places.

Downtown Tokyo was completely destroyed. The Ginza area was pretty well wiped out. I saw people fleeing, their faces covered with soot, their clothing torn off. It was happening almost every night. We had some shelters, but they were so primitive they couldn't do any good.

I studied at the Tokyo University Law School for one month, and then in May '45 I was sent to a navy factory outside the city. It was just three months before the end. There wasn't enough material to work on, so we ended up as farmers, growing potatoes and pumpkins. Before the pumpkins grew big enough to eat, the war ended. (Laughs.)

We knew we were losing the war. First we lost Guadalcanal and then we lost Saipan. The government was saying we weren't losing the islands, we were just retreating strategically. We didn't believe them. They were hiding the bad news. We didn't know that the Imperial Japanese Fleet had by this time been ninety percent destroyed. We thought it was still intact, hiding somewhere. There were some **diehards**,[3] hoping, lying to themselves, but most of us were having doubts.

At first it was hush-hush. Nobody dared express his doubts. We knew that life was getting more and more miserable. We didn't have enough to eat. We didn't even have rice. Without rice, life means nothing. (Laughs.) We were eating all sorts of junk, like seaweed, the kind we would never touch. We were eating awful fish we had never heard of. (Laughs.) Everybody was getting thin and losing much weight. The American planes were dropping leaflets from the sky: The war will be over soon. If you don't surrender now, we may have to drop more bombs on Tokyo.

We didn't know what to expect from the Americans. The hard-core **militarists**[4] were warning us that all our men would be made into slaves, would be sent to China to do hard labor, and all our women would be made prostitutes. It was a great relief when the Americans came and no such things happened. (Laughs.)

The day after Hiroshima was bombed, there was a headline telling us about a special bomb. They didn't say "atomic bomb" because they didn't know what

---

[3] **diehards**—those who are stubborn and resist change.
[4] **militarists**—those who strongly support the war and fighting.

it was. They said it was extremely powerful and a tremendous number of people were killed. We were all discussing it: What is this thing? It was a scary feeling.

I remember August 15, 1945. I got the day off from my farm work to go to Tokyo for some dental treatment. A friend and I listened to the radio broadcast by the Emperor, announcing the end of the war. He was using all kinds of highfalutin' expressions to make things sound vague, but we realized that Japan had surrendered. We were very sad, but at the same time we both had a tremendous sense of relief. We felt we had suffered enough and things had to change. There was a naval base right near the factory where we worked. Some fanatical officers wanted to fight on. To lose honorably: to die fighting. They were exhorting everybody and getting nowhere.

I got back to Tokyo ten days after the war. When winter came, we were really miserable. We had neither food nor clothing. There wasn't anything to eat in Tokyo, so they closed the university for two months. They declared a winter vacation. (Laughs.) We were told to go to the countryside and find food wherever we could. There was nothing in Tokyo.

The liberal professors, who had been fired during the war by the military powers, came back. There was a feeling of freedom we hadn't enjoyed before. Strange as it may sound, the Emperor's speech had a tremendous influence on everybody. He said we had to fight this war, of course. But now that it was over, we had to usher in a new era of peace and rebuild our country. People had to believe the war was not in vain in order to live on.

We still didn't have enough food or clothing. Very few of the university students could afford the black school uniforms. Many had returned from the war and were still wearing soldiers' uniforms to class.

The Occupation forces began distributing American food to the Japanese people. Everything was rationed, and we stood in line. We sometimes received American potatoes and we couldn't believe how huge they were. (Laughs.) Japanese potatoes are much, much smaller. These were two, three times as large. The canned goods may not have been great by American standards, but to us everything tasted great.

One day I saw a group of American soldiers marching along the street. It was about two weeks after the war. It was the first time I had ever seen American soldiers. I remember clearly how scared stiff they were, too. They didn't know what to expect either. They thought there might still be some fanatics around. We were scared stiff because we thought maybe these soldiers would do something wild. They were such young boys. These scary moments were over quickly when we learned they were okay and they learned that the Japanese were quite peaceful now. Of course. We were so tired of fighting, we had no energy left. (Laughs.)

After the war, when a lot of Americans came to Japan, they all looked so well-fed and well-dressed, so healthy. In contrast to us, who were all emaciated. That was the first thing that hit us so hard. We said to ourselves, Why did we fight these people? We couldn't have won. (Laughs.) They brought all kinds of food and equipment and were building all over Japan. They even erected some American villages, naming them Washington Heights, Grant Heights, Jackson Heights. (Laughs.) These places were so different from where we lived in Tokyo. We didn't have enough electricity or gas. They were living in absolute luxury. Two or three hours a night, we had electricity. The rest of time we used candles. They were using electricity like water. There was some resentment, of course.

One nice thing came out of the war. I met my wife. Her father was a U.S. Army chaplain who came to Japan in 1948. His wife and my aunt had attended Mount

Holyoke College way back. Our family was a very academic one. Most of us turned pro-American, a feeling that had been suppressed during the war.

JOHN KENNETH GALBRAITH
Economist, memoirist, former ambassador to India.

The great principle of American war strategy is: We have airplanes, therefore they must be effective.

Sometime in 1944, Roosevelt came to the conclusion that there was a large element of exaggeration and pure guesswork in what the air force was accomplishing. He responded to several suggestions that there should be an independent civilian commission established, to go with the troops as they moved into France and Germany to find out what really happened.

In the spring of 1945, I was brought into this by George Ball and Paul Nitze. The three of us formed the core of the operation under Henry Alexander, who came in from J. P. Morgan and Company. It had the advantage that you operated well out of the range of guns. Quite a few people find this advantageous in war, including some generals.

The results were not in doubt. The bombing of Germany both by the British and ourselves had far less effect than was thought at the time. The German arms industry continued to expand its output until the autumn of 1944, in spite of the heaviest air attacks. Some of the best-publicized attacks, including those on German ball-bearing plants, practically grounded the Eighth Air Force for months. Its losses were that heavy. At the end of the war, the Germans had ball bearings for export again. Our attacks on their air-frame plants were a total failure. In the months after the great spring raids of 1944, their production increased by big amounts.

The reasons were threefold. First, the machine tools were relatively invulnerable. They'd be buried under rubble but could be dug out in a day or two. Second, it was possible to decentralize production: to move the machinery into schools and churches. It was reorganized in much less time than was imagined. The Germans discovered that it wasn't necessary for production to be in a single factory. They also discovered a large range of substitutes. It was possible to redesign a lot of equipment to reduce the use of ball bearings. Third, it was possible to reorganize what had been sporadic and less than diligent managements.

The most disappointing of the attacks was on the airplane plants. Production was taken away from Hermann Goering, who was expansively incompetent, and put in the Speer ministry, which was much better. This more than offset the damage done by the bombers.

A similar case was in the bombing of Hamburg. It destroyed the center of the city and made available a large number of people—restaurant workers, cabaret performers, bankers, teachers, salesmen. They all became available as a working force in the war plants at the edge of the city.

There had been two broad strategies. The British bombed at night and went for the central cities, because that was all they could find. Naturally, working-class areas were the most damaged. The middle classes lived on the outskirts and were hardly touched. This was true of most cities, ours and theirs. In general, poor people lived in the center and the **affluent**[5] lived on the edges. It was the East End of London that was hardest hit by the Luftwaffe. Or a working-class city like Coventry. The same thing went for German cities.

American strategy involved daylight raids. We aimed for the plants themselves. The problem was targeting. In a large number of cases, we couldn't hit them.

---

[5] **affluent**—people who are wealthy or rich, the upper class.

There was a saying in 1945: We made a major onslaught on German agriculture.

I don't want to exaggerate. Some of the big plants were hit. One in central Germany, which produced synthetic fuels, was hit repeatedly. The attacks on the German oil supply had a considerable effect on the mobility of their ground forces. They were only successful because it was an enormous plant covering acres and acres. And we hit it repeatedly. The Germans had some hundreds of thousands of people at work repairing that plant all the time.

The war for other people ended in the summer of 1945. For us, it continued on through that autumn in a major row with the air force. Naturally, they were far from enchanted with our figures as they became available. The instinct of the air force was first to deny the figures and then to suppress them.

The over-all conclusion was that wars were won by the slogging progress of the troops across France and into Germany, with a good deal of help from tactical air power: support for the actual movement of troops on the ground. It was an extended form of artillery. Strategic bombing was designed to destroy the industrial base of the enemy and the morale of its people. It did neither.

Need I say that this conclusion was less than popular at the time?

What about the fire bombings of Tokyo?

We concluded that, on the whole, the Japanese industry did not have the same recovery capacity as the German. When the Japanese war plants were hit, they were more likely to stay out of production. You have to remember that from 1941 to 1945, Japan was a very small country with an equally small industrial base. It was stretched very tight and had little of the resilience of the German economy.

Yet the fire bombing of Japanese cities was not a decisive factor in the war. The war in Asia was won by the hard, slow progress up from the south and across the Pacific.

All of war is cruel and unnecessary, but the bombings made this one especially so. The destruction of Dresden was unforgivable. It was done very late in the war, as part of a military dynamic which was out of control and had no relationship to any military needs.

Didn't the dropping of the A-bomb on Hiroshima and Nagasaki shorten the Pacific war?

The bomb did not end the Japanese war. This was something that was carefully studied by our bombing survey. Paul Nitze headed it in Japan, so there was hardly any bias in this matter. It's ironic that he has since become fascinated with the whole culture of destruction. The conclusion of the monograph called *Japan's Struggle to End the War* was that it was a difference, at most, of two or three weeks. The decision had already been taken to get out of the war, to seek a peace negotiation.

The Japanese government, at that time, was heavily bureaucratic. The decision took some time to translate into action. There was also a fear that some of the army units might go in for a kind of Kamikaze resistance. The decision was not known in Washington. While the bomb did not bring an end to the war, one cannot say Washington ordered the attacks in the knowledge that the war was coming to an end.

Would not millions have been lost, American and Japanese, in the projected attack on the mainland, had it not been for the bomb?

That is not true. There would have been negotiations for surrender within days or a few weeks under any circumstances. Before the A-bombs were dropped, Japan was a defeated nation. This was realized.

This experience, as a member of the commission, had an enormous effect on my attitudes. You had to see these German cities, city after city, in 1945 and then go on to the utter horror of Japanese cities to see how frightful modern air warfare is. There is nothing nice about ground warfare: twenty thousand men were killed on the first day in the Battle of the Somme in World War One. But this didn't have the high visibility of Berlin, Frankfurt, Cologne, Mainz. And to see Tokyo leveled to the ground. I was left with an image which has stayed with me all of my life.

QUESTIONS TO CONSIDER

1. How did Akira Miuri feel about the end of the war and the American occupation of Japan?

2. What does Galbraith feel was the main problem in using airpower during World War II?

3. Does Galbraith's account of a Japan near surrender in the summer of 1945 agree or disagree with Miuri's description of Japan around the time of the Hiroshima bombing? Cite details from Miuri's part of the selection to support your answer.

Preparing the Bomb

▲

J. Robert Oppenheimer and General Groves General Leslie
Groves directed the Manhattan Project, in which the first atomic
bomb was developed. Robert Oppenheimer, shown in civilian clothes,
directed the scientific team at Los Alamos. Here Oppenheimer
and Groves inspect the site of one of the first atomic bomb tests near
Alamogordo, New Mexico.

Alamogordo The test on July 16, 1945, in Alamogardo, New Mexico,
of the atomic bomb was the first of several critical steps in its
development. The building of the atomic bomb required the joint work
of thousands and was a marvel of scientific collaboration.

▲

Paul Tibbets The pilot of the first atomic bombing mission was Colonel Paul Tibbets.

"Enola Gay" The plane that dropped the first atomic bomb in the history of warfare was named the "Enola Gay," after the mother of the pilot, Colonel Paul Tibetts. ▶

▲

Loading the Bomb Loading the atomic bomb was a delicate operation in itself. The first bomb weighed about 9,000 pounds.

Weighty Problem Because of the enormous weight of the bomb, it was loaded into the Enola Gay with a lift from below.

A large team of mechanics, technicians, and scientists was required to complete the assembly.

▼

▲

Hiroshima The first atomic bomb dropped over Hiroshima, called
"Little Boy," weighed more than 9,000 pounds. It was 28 inches in diameter and 120 inches long. It used uranium to trigger its blast. Its explosive
impact was like that of approximately 15,000 tons of explosives.

Nagasaki Nicknamed "Fat Boy," the atomic bomb dropped over
Nagasaki weighed nearly 10,000 pounds and was 60 inches in diameter
and 128 inches long. Because it used plutonium, it had a greater
explosive impact than "Little Boy."

▼

Hiroshima and Nagasaki

"A White Light and a Black Rain"

BY JOSEPH L. MARX

Forty-three seconds after the atomic bomb nicknamed "Little Boy" slipped out of the Enola Gay, it exploded 2,000 feet above Hiroshima. Said Robert Lewis, the co-pilot of the mission, "I don't believe anyone ever expected to look at a sight quite like that. Where we had seen a clear city two minutes before, we could now no longer see the city. We could see smoke and fires creeping up the sides of the mountains." Here historian Joseph Marx describes the effect of the explosion on Hiroshima in his book Seven Hours to Zero.

The people of Hiroshima were blinded by a flash of light. Unlike the men on the *Enola Gay,* they had not expected it.

There was no sound connected with the flash of pure light. The men on the plane heard nothing resembling an explosion and the people in Hiroshima do not remember hearing any noise at all. A fisherman some distance away on the Inland Sea, however, saw the flash and heard the roar of an explosion. Though he was at least twenty miles from Hiroshima, he reported that the sound of that single **detonation**[1] was greater than that of B-29s bombing a town only five miles away.

In Hiroshima only a few people had bothered to look up when they heard the high-flying planes. They could not see the bomb but they witnessed a strange maneuver. One plane peeled off to the right, the other to the left. Then there was a sudden blossoming of three parachutes as the instruments were released from *The Great Artiste.* Some of the on-lookers, thinking the parachutes signified trouble aboard one of the planes, cheered. To have survived the event they witnessed, these viewers had to have been some distance away. The flash of light, one-third of a mile above the city, was visual evidence of an **unprecedented**[2] man-made blast of heat. Anyone near ground zero (that part of the earth directly below the point of detonation) was instantly and totally incinerated.

The results of the detonation of the atomic bomb on Hiroshima came in stages. First there was the incredible flash of light when the two small masses of uranium-235 got together, became critical and released, in a split second, a fantastic amount of heat and radiation. Immediately, or in a few seconds after the flash (depending on the distance from ground zero), there was a crushing impact of the **concussion**[3] caused by this violent release of energy. Then there were fires, the great wind and the fire storm.

The effect of the sudden blast of millions of degrees of heat was stunning. People and objects simply vanished. Some left their shadows imprinted in stone. Tiles in the

---

[1] **detonation**—an explosion with a loud noise.

[2] **unprecedented**—never done before.

[3] **concussion**—sudden, violent shaking or shock.

roofs simply dissolved if they were within six hundred yards of ground zero. Mica **fused**[4] into granite gravestones. People farther away and not protected from the direct heat rays were burned. The gravity of a burn depended on the man's distance from the source. The mayor of Kobe, a town ten miles away, saw the flash and felt the heat on his face. People as far as two and a half miles away were burned on their bare skin.

Those who were wearing white clothes were spared the more severe burns if they were some distance from ground zero. The difference between the heat-absorbing characteristic of dark colors and the heat-repelling trait of white was graphically illustrated on people's skin. Women some distance from ground zero, wearing patterned dresses and **kimonos**,[5] showed the patterns on their bodies, which were burned in the design of what they were wearing. Often, if any clothing was left on them, it was the white portion. The dark parts were burned away and the skin below was badly burned, the extent of the burn varying with the shadings of the pattern. On the pages of an open book, some distance away, the blank paper seemed untouched, but all the letters had been neatly burned out.

To be burned by the heat, a person not too close to ground zero had to be in a direct line with the source. A man could have a serious burn on one side of his face or body and none on the other. People had burned and unburned patterns on their bodies showing what had been protected and what exposed. The extra thickness of a shirt collar might leave a band of light around a man's neck and a fold of fat might leave a clear crease in his stomach. The surface color of stone was altered by the fusing of certain elements in the rock. Protected areas, however, were not changed, and the result is what has been called "shadows in stone."

---

[4] **fused**—melted through intense heat.

[5] **kimonos**—loose, outer garments worn by Japanese men and women.

Those who were in the immediate area of the target (Second Imperial Army Headquarters) had little chance to do anything. Almost all who were not vaporized by the heat were killed by impact and radiation. The roofs of "fireproof" buildings close to ground zero were driven through successive floors and into the ground. Stone pillars near the center of the blast were driven straight down into the earth. The damage done by fire and blast cannot be blamed on the traditional Japanese construction. The building laws had been changed after the 1923 earthquake, and the roofs of new buildings had to be able to support a minimum load of 70 pounds per square foot. (American building-code specifications rarely go beyond 40.) No one was anticipating the 1,800-pound pressure exerted by the blast at Hiroshima.

Nor could anyone anticipate the type of heat developed by the bomb. Generally heat develops in stages, builds up to its height, and then dies down. In this instance, the heat was, literally, a flash—a brief, momentary blast that seared everything within range and then was gone, leaving only its effects.

The wave of heat started a multitude of fires beyond the areas where it burned everything to a crisp. The blast and later wind augmented the fires. Charcoal braziers, still hot from breakfast cooking, started more fires when buildings collapsed from the blast. Even if the fire department had managed to remain intact, it would have been ineffective. Fire trucks could not have passed through the streets and in a large area no streets remained. The blast caused 70,000 water-main breaks, which meant that almost all the water in the affected area had to come from wells.

The fires that had started from the heat of the blast, from overturned cooking stoves or from mangled electric supply lines, grew and fed on themselves. As the hot air rose into the tremendous mushroom cloud, it pulled in more air from outside the area, feeding fresh oxygen to the flames. The combination of the blast and wind and collapsing buildings brought another danger—flying glass. There was hardly an unbroken windowpane in Hiroshima except at the edges of the city, and flying shards of glass were a major cause of casualties. The fire storm actually created a "twister," an American-style, funnel-shaped tornado that finally blew itself out to sea as a waterspout.

The reports of the survivors vary. Eye-witnesses agree on only two points: the lack of an explosive sound and the astonishing, dazzling burst of light that seemed to flash from east to west. After that, the reports differ according to the person who gave it, what he was doing, and where he was.

The flash seemed to **permeate**[6] everything—houses, buildings, even caves. The wave of pressure followed it. While the detonation seemed to be noiseless to those nearby (the sudden pressure may have been too much for their eardrums), the sound of the collapsing buildings was heard all over. Nearby survivors thought they had escaped a bomb that had scored a near miss. This was a fairly universal thought. In the same way that every man on the *Enola Gay* thought that flak had burst near his own position when the shock wave hit, the survivors of Hiroshima thought a bomb had exploded just above or next to them.

The disaster at Hiroshima caused an odd sort of traffic into and out of the city. People outside the target area, knowing that something had happened in Hiroshima, started in toward the center of the town. Moving toward the city out of curiosity or a desire to help or to find their families, they were met by a stream of **refugees**[7] blindly fleeing the scene of trouble. The refugees walked without life and without goal. They walked only to get away

---

[6] **permeate**—to soak through or spread through the whole of something.

[7] **refugees**—persons who are fleeing for safety, often out of a country during war or after a natural disaster.

from where they had been. Some walked with one or both arms upraised in an effort to keep burned arms away from burned bodies.

Many were hideously burned in a manner that became recognizable. Their skin had been so badly seared by the flash that it peeled away, leaving the victims featureless. Possibly the most gruesome sight was witnessed by a Japanese priest who encountered a group of about twenty soldiers. They had been part of an antiaircraft battery, far enough from ground zero that they had not been killed instantly. They must have been looking up toward the planes when the detonation came. Their faces were wholly burned and their eye sockets were hollow. The fluid from their eyeballs had melted and run down their cheeks.

Many of the people of Hiroshima who were uninjured or whose injuries were comparatively minor tried to flee to the foothills. Those who remained in the battered city made their way to various open spaces, islands and parade grounds, that had been set aside as shelter areas. These quickly became overcrowded with injured, dying, and comparatively healthy people who had no place else to go.

The intense heat started immediate fires. The pressure wave knocked down buildings, causing and spreading more fires. Over it all rose a cloud composed of dust, ashes, pieces of buildings and land and debris of all kinds, bringing an almost nighttime darkness to the morning.

The heat created by the atomic fireball and fire storm sucked the sea-level atmosphere upward. As it reached the cooler levels of the upper atmosphere, the moist air condensed and some of it fell back to earth in the form of rain. It was not a normal rain but a downpour of huge black drops of water as large as marbles. This black rain, noticed by so many survivors, picked up its coloring matter on the way down when it passed through the cloud of dust and ashes.

The people of Hiroshima did not, of course, realize that they had been hit by an atomic bomb. Some, who had seen the parachutes and the flash of light, thought it had been a magnesium bomb set off in the air above them. Rumors and theories spread. One was that the city had been sprayed with gasoline and then set afire by a magnesium bomb. Another was that a form of poisonous gas had been used. There was a peculiar smell in the air, and many people who died seemed to have suffered no injuries, at least nothing that should have been fatal. It wasn't until later that doctors realized these people had died of radiation poisoning.

The **fission**[8] of the small amount of uranium in Little Boy threw off neutrons, beta particles, and gamma rays. Too many of these, bombarding the human body, change the cell structure. Depending on the number absorbed and other factors, they either kill the recipient or make him sick.

That was one of the reasons the bomb was detonated almost 2,000 feet above the target. The test at Alamogordo indicated that the earth and objects quite a distance from ground zero became radioactive and remained that way for some time. The Army was not looking for damage by radiation but by heat and blast, so it was decided to detonate the bomb about one-third of a mile above the earth. Despite this precaution, doctors estimated that radiation had killed ninety-five percent of the people within half a mile of ground zero at Hiroshima. The medical men realized later that many of those who had suffered from serious burns and blast effects had not been killed by them but by radiation.

The doctors came to divide the radiation sickness into three stages. The first stage usually came fairly soon after exposure. The symptoms were nausea, headaches, diarrhea, fever, and **torpor**.[9] The second stage developed

---

[8] **fission**—a splitting apart, division into parts.

[9] **torpor**—dullness, listlessness, lack of energy or movement.

ten to fifteen days after the detonation and was recognized by falling hair and a fever that might reach as high as 106 degrees. The third stage came twenty-five to thirty days after the explosion and was characterized by blood disorders. There was bleeding from the gums and other places, and there were skin sores. There was also a sharp drop in the white blood-cell count.

This lowering of the white cell count left the patient less capable of resisting infection, and wounds that had begun to heal would cease to heal and become infected. In most of the radiation-sickness patients the white blood-cell count dropped from a normal 6,000 or 7,000 to below 4,000. If it continued to go down and went to 1,000 or below, the patient died. Similarly, a fever that did not fluctuate but remained high for any length of time was a sign of fatality. Some victims recovered in a week. Some took several months.

Various peculiarities showed up among the wounded. Most of the bad burns healed with deep layers of pink, rubbery scar tissue. People who had suffered direct burns from the heat were protected to a certain extent from radiation sickness. Those who had lain quietly for a few days, or even several hours, after the bombing, were not as apt to get sick as those who had been active. Gray hair didn't fall out as readily as black hair. The reproductive organs were affected, and men and women became temporarily sterile.

The scientists at Los Alamos saw the effect of too much radiation in their laboratories. Harry Daghlian, the young Purdue physicist who watched and helped Dr. Slotin "tickle the dragon's tail," received a fatal dose of radioactivity. His hands swelled, his skin fell away in patches from his body, his white blood-cell count dropped dramatically, and on August 21, 1945, he died.

The following day, Dr. Slotin, still experimenting with his silvery hemispheres of plutonium, lost control of the screwdriver he was holding. The tool slipped and the two bright pieces of **plutonium**[10] came together in a sudden embrace that would begin a chain reaction. Dr. Slotin hastily tore the two pieces of metal apart with his bare hands. Then, knowing that he had no chance of surviving, he went to the blackboard and sketched the position of the accident and the places of all the men in the room so that their distances from the source of the rays could be determined and the laboratory's doctors could check on the amount of radiation they had received. Dr. Slotin died within ten days.

In Hiroshima, there was a rumor that the city would be radioactive and that no one would be able to live there for years. But less than two weeks after the detonation, scientists went over the area with instruments and discovered that even at ground zero the radiation level was not much higher than normal.

The statisticians went to work at once. The first figures showed that 78,150 people had been killed, 13,938 were missing, and that 37,425 had been injured. These early figures were accepted by the United States government as official, but as time went on more bodies were discovered and urns containing ashes remained unclaimed. The statisticians then estimated that at least 100,000 people, mostly civilians, had been killed. The causes of death were less clear. Many people whose deaths had been attributed to radiation may have actually been stunned into a near-**catatonic**[11] state by the tragedy. But the public-health authorities estimated that about twenty-five percent of the deaths came as a result of direct burns, twenty percent from radiation effects, and more than fifty percent from other injuries, among which flying glass was quite prominent. But as the deaths and injuries often came from a combination of causes, these figures are, at best, little more than well-informed guesses.

---

[10] **plutonium**—an element important in creating atomic fission.

[11] **catatonic**—a state in which a person is unable to speak or move, except for occasional outbursts or seizures.

The figures on property damage, however, were much more precise. Out of 90,000 buildings, 62,000 had been destroyed and 6,000 had been damaged beyond repair. In the heart of the city, only five modern buildings were in good enough condition to be used without complete rebuilding or major repairs. The percentage in the suburbs was naturally higher. Some comparatively nearby buildings were protected from heat or blast by hills while others, much farther away, were in a direct line with the point of detonation.

What had been a functioning city had been instantly transformed into almost complete and total chaos.

After looking at the results of the detonation, Captain Lewis wrote in his journal: "I am certain the entire crew felt this experience was more than any human had thought possible. It just seems impossible to comprehend. I have the feeling of groping for words to explain this. . . ."

QUESTIONS TO CONSIDER

1. What are the 3 or 4 major stages of the atomic bomb's detonation?

2. What things accounted for the great differences in the burns and injuries that the people of Hiroshima received?

3. Why was "Little Boy" detonated 2,000 feet above ground?

4. Is the atomic bomb in your opinion more or less terrible than other weapons? Why?

Hiroshima and Nagasaki: Injuries to the Human Body

BY THE COMMITTEE FOR THE COMPILATION[1] OF MATERIALS ON DAMAGE CAUSED BY THE ATOMIC BOMBS

In 1976, thirty-four Japanese scientists and physicians formed the Committee for the Compilation of Materials on the Damage Caused by the Atomic Bombs. This committee created the most comprehensive survey on the effects of the atomic bombings ever done. Published in 1981, the study documents statistically the physical, medical, and social damage created by the two atomic bombings.

---

[1] **compilation**—act of pulling or putting together from several sources.

Total Number of Casualties due to the Atomic Bomb, Hiroshima, 10 August, 1946*

Distance from Hypocenter (km)	Severely Killed	Slightly Injured	Injured	Not Missing	Injured	Total
Under 0.5	19,329	478	338	593	924	21,662
0.5-1.0	42,271	3,046	1,919	1,366	4,434	53,036
1.0-1.5	37,689	7,732	9,522	1,188	9,140	65,271
1.5-2.0	13,422	7,627	11,516	227	11,698	44,490
2.0-2.5	4,513	7,830	14,149	98	26,096	52,686
2.5-3.0	1,139	2,923	6,795	32	19,907	30,796
3.0-3.5	117	474	1,934	2	10,250	12,777
3.5-4.0	100	295	1,768	3	13,513	15,679
4.0-4.5	8	64	373		4,260	4,705
4.5-5.0	31	36	156	1	6,593	6,817
Over 5.0	42	19	136	167	11,798	12,162
Total	118,661	30,524	48,606	3,677	118,613	320,081

*Military personnel not included.

Source: Hiroshima Shiyakusho, *Hiroshima Genbaku Sensaishi* [RHAWD], (Hiroshima, 1971). vol. I.

Number of Casualties due to the Atomic Bomb in Nagasaki* as of 31 December 1945

Killed	73,884
Injured	74,909
Affected	120,820

*It is unknown whether floating population, such as military personnel and other volunteer corps, is included. Source: Nagasaki City A-bomb Records Preservation Committee.

According to the results obtained from observations made on atomic bomb injury from a medical standpoint, the general course of this condition in those exposed can be divided into the following four stages, as abstracted from the Summary Report of Investigation of Atomic Bomb Casualties:

1. Stage 1—Early or Initial Stage

The greatest number of casualties occurred immediately after the explosion to the end of the second week; and at this stage various injurious actions of the atomic bomb explosion simultaneously led to the onset of symptoms. Approximately nine tenths of the fatal cases died during this stage, and the majority (about 90 percent) of these injured who received medical care for several days after the explosion complained of **thermal**[2] injury.

2. Stage 2—Intermittent[3] Stage

Many moderate injuries caused by radioactivity were encountered from the beginning of the third week to the end of the eighth week; and the remaining fatal cases, or one tenth, died. From the general course taken by the victims, stages 1 and 2 may be considered as the acute stage of atomic bomb injury.

3. Stage 3—Late Stage

From the beginning of the third month to the end of the fourth, all symptoms from injury showed some improvement, although a few cases terminated in death from complications. By the end of the fourth month (early December 1945), those suffering from the disaster in both cities had recovered to a certain degree, and the course of the atomic bomb injury itself had come to a near end.

4. Stage 4—Delayed Effects

After five months or more, there were various delayed effects: some—such as distortion, **contracture**,[4] **keloid**,[5] and so on—following recovery from thermal

---

[2] **thermal**—of or related to heat, created or caused by heat.

[3] **intermittent**—starting and stopping.

[4] **contracture**—permanent shortening of scar tissue that results in deformity.

[5] **keloid**—a red, raised formation of scar tissue.

injury or mechanical injury; some—such as **anemia**[6]—as a result of blood disorder caused by radiation injury; and some originating in disturbances of the reproductive function—such as **sterility**[7]—may occur at this stage. There are, however, not a few items that must be continuously examined during the following few months.

These categories of atomic bomb injury summarize the many medical observations made at that period and reflect the actual conditions of the exposed. In reality, however, these stages were not the end of the injury to the human body following the explosion; and various delayed effects began to appear after certain periods of latency. Even today, more than thirty years since the explosion, these effects have not come to an end. The first case of atomic bomb cataract in Hiroshima was discovered in the autumn of 1948, and this was followed by many reports on this condition in both cities. Leukemia in those exposed to the atomic bomb first appeared in 1945 in Nagasaki and in 1946 in Hiroshima. Its incidence rose gradually thereafter, reached its peak between 1950 and 1953, and has maintained its high percentage ever since. Slightly after the peak of leukemia, a general trend in the increase of various cancers (thyroid, breast, lung, and salivary gland cancer) was found among the exposed. Microcephaly and developmental disturbances were encountered among infants exposed in utero,[8] and these conditions were studied for genetic effects. If injuries to the body immediately after the explosion and those up to six months after it, and also their direct aftereffects are to be called atomic bomb injuries *of the acute stage*, late effects may be called atomic bomb injuries *of the late stage*. Fortunately investigations to date have revealed no harmful genetic effects in either the first filial

---

[6] **anemia**—a lack of red blood cells, resulting in weakness and causing tiredness and inability to fight infection.

[7] **sterility**—inability to have children, not able to reproduce.

[8] in utero—when an infant is still in the mother's womb during pregnancy.

generation (F_1) or the second filial generation (F_2), but further investigations and studies on atomic bomb illness must be continued for several generations to come.

Atomic bomb illness not only is a **pathological**[9] condition that the human race has confronted for the first time but also possesses a specific characteristic unlike the usual war damage and injury. In the first place, the energy causing vital damage is vast. Not until August in the year of 1945 had mankind ever experienced large-scale thermal radiation and blast; and, together with radioactivity, these caused the deaths of 140,000 in Hiroshima and 70,000 in Nagasaki. In the second place, atomic bomb illness is the first and only example of heavy lethal and momentary doses of whole body **irradiation**.[10] It destroyed the actively regenerating cells in the body and greatly devastated the vital defensive mechanism. These heavy doses were the main reason for the poor repair, the prevalence of infection, and the extremely high mortality in atomic bomb injury. The atomic bomb not only brought tragic and horrible injuries to the exposed but also hindered the basis for the **reparative**[11] and regenerative processes of the living body. Thirdly, whole body irradiation injured the nuclei of the cells and their component DNA (deoxyribonucleic acid) and may lead to the induction of malignancies (cancer and leukemia) and to alteration of genes. One should never forget that such momentary injurious action of an atomic bomb can have aftereffects for years and generations to come. We should look squarely at the facts and bear the heart-heavy responsibility for seeing that such a disaster will never again befall the human race.

---

[9] **pathological**—resulting from a disease.

[10] **irradiation**—intense dose of radiation.

[11] **reparative**—ability to repair or heal.

QUESTIONS TO CONSIDER

1. What are the immediate medical aftereffects of the atomic bomb?

2. What are the long-term signs of "atomic bomb illness"?

3. Do you think that the aftereffects of the atomic bomb make it more than just a military weapon?

Hiroshima: The Victims

**BY FLETCHER KNEBEL AND
CHARLES W. BAILEY II**

*From a variety of sources, historians have pieced together the
story of what happened on August 6 in Hiroshima. Here historians
Knebel and Bailey peer into the lives of Hiroshima residents just
moments before the blast. The result is an account that reads
more like a novel than history.*

The sounding of the all-clear signal in Hiroshima at
7:13 A.M. on August 6 made little change in the tempo of
the city. Most people had been too busy, or too lazy, to
pay much attention to the alert. The departure of the
single, high-flying B-29 caused no more stir than its
arrival over the city twenty-two minutes earlier.

As the plane flew out over the sea, Michiyoshi
Nukushina, a thirty-eight-year-old fire-truck driver at
the Hiroshima Army Ordnance Supply Depot, climbed

onto his bicycle and headed for home. He had received special permission to quit his post half an hour before his shift ended. Wearing an official-duty armband to clear himself through the depot gates, and carrying a new pair of wooden clogs and a bag of fresh tomatoes drawn from the depot commissary, he headed home through the narrow streets of Hiroshima.

Nukushina crossed two of the seven river channels that divided the city into fingerlike islands and finally arrived at his home in Kakomachi precinct a little more than half an hour after leaving the firehouse. Propping his bicycle by an entrance to his small combination home and wineshop he walked inside and called to his wife to go get the tomatoes.

At this same instant, in a comfortable house behind the high hill that made Hijiyama Park a welcome variation in the otherwise flat terrain of Hiroshima, a mother named Chinayo Sakamoto was mopping her kitchen floor after breakfast. Her son Tsuneo, an Army captain fortunately stationed right in his home town, had left for duty with his unit. His wife Miho had gone upstairs. Tsuneo's father lay on the straw mat in the living room, reading his morning paper.

Off to the east and south of the city, a few men in air defense posts were watching the morning sky or listening to their sound-detection equipment. At the Matsunaga lookout station, in the hills east of Hiroshima, a watcher filed two reports with the air defense center. At 8:06, he sighted and reported two planes, headed northwest. At 8:09, he saw another, following some miles behind them, and corrected his report to include it.

At 8:14, the telephone talker at the Nakano searchlight battery also made a report. His sound equipment had picked up the noise of aircraft engines. Unidentified planes were coming from Saijo, about fifteen miles east of Hiroshima, and were heading toward the city.

The anti-aircraft gunners on Mukay-Shima Island in Hiroshima harbor could now see two planes, approaching the eastern edge of the city at very high altitude. As they watched, at precisely seventeen seconds after 8:15, the planes suddenly separated. The leading aircraft made a tight, diving turn to the right. The second plane performed an identical maneuver to the left, and from it fell three parachutes which opened and floated slowly down toward the city.

The few people in Hiroshima who caught sight of the two planes saw the parachutes blossom as the aircraft turned away from the city. Some cheered when they saw them, thinking the enemy planes must be in trouble and the crews were starting to bail out.

For three quarters of a minute there was nothing in the clear sky over the city except the parachutes and the diminishing whine of airplane engines as the B-29's retreated into the lovely blue morning.

Then suddenly, without a sound, there was no sky left over Hiroshima.

For those who were there and who survived to recall the moment when man first turned on himself the elemental forces of his own universe, the first instant was pure light, blinding, intense light, but light of an awesome beauty and variety.

In the pause between detonation and impact, a pause that for some was so short it could not register on the senses, but which for others was long enough for shock to give way to fear and for fear in turn to yield to instinctive efforts at self-preservation, the sole impression was visual. If there was sound, no one heard it.

To Nukushina, just inside his house, and to Mrs. Sakamoto, washing her kitchen floor, it was simply sudden and complete blackness.

For Nukushina's wife, reaching for the bag of tomatoes on her husband's bicycle, it was a blue flash streaking across her eyes.

For Dr. Imagawa, at his patient's city home, it again was darkness. For his wife, in the suburban hills to the west, it was a "rainbow-colored object," whirling horizontally across the sky over the city.

To Yuko Yamaguchi, cleaning up after breakfast in the rented farmhouse where she and her in-laws now lived, it was a sudden choking black cloud as the accumulated **soot**[1] and grime of decades seemed to leap from the old walls.

Hayano Susukida, bent over to pick up a salvaged roof tile so she could pass it down the line of "volunteer" workers, did not see anything. She was merely crushed to the ground as if by some monstrous supernatural hand. But her son Junichiro, lounging outside his dormitory at Otake, saw a flash that turned from white to pink and then to blue as it rose and blossomed. Others, also at a distance of some miles, seemed to see "five or six bright colors." Some saw merely "flashes of gold" in a white light that reminded them—this was perhaps the most common description—of a huge photographic flashbulb exploding over the city.

The duration of this curiously detached spectacle varied with the distance of the viewer from the point in mid-air where the two lumps of U-235 were driven together inside the bomb. It did not last more than a few seconds at the most.

For thousands in Hiroshima it did not last even that long, if in fact there was any moment of grace at all. They were simply burned black and dead where they stood by the radiant heat that turned central Hiroshima into a gigantic oven. For thousands of others there was perhaps a second or two, certainly not long enough for wonder or terror or even recognition of things seen but not believed, before they were shredded by the thousands of pieces of shattered window glass that flew

---

[1] **soot**—the black substance in the smoke made from burning coal, wood, or oil.

before the blast waves or were crushed underneath walls, beams, bricks, or any other solid object that stood in the way of the explosion.

For everyone else in history's first atomic target, the initial assault on the visual sense was followed by an instinctive assumption that a very large bomb had scored a direct hit on or near the spot where they were standing.

Old Mr. Sakamoto, who a moment before had been lounging on the living-room floor with his newspaper, found himself standing barefoot in his back yard, the paper still in his hand. Then his wife staggered out of the house, and perhaps half a minute later, his daughter-in-law Miho, who had been upstairs, groped her way out also.

Dr. Imagawa had just reached for his medical satchel to begin the examination of his patient. When the blackness lifted from his senses, he found himself standing on top of a five-foot pile of rubble that had been the sickroom. With him, surprisingly, were both the sick man and the patient's young son.

Mrs. Susukida, flat on the ground amid the pile of old roof tiles, was left all but naked, stripped of every piece of outer clothing and now wearing only her underwear, which itself was badly torn.

Mrs. Nukushina had just time to throw her hands over her eyes after she saw the blue flash. Then she was knocked insensible. When she recovered consciousness, she lay in what seemed to her to be utter darkness. All around her there was only rubble where a moment earlier there had been her home and her husband's bicycle and the bag of fresh tomatoes. She too was now without clothing except for her underwear. Her body was rapidly becoming covered with her own blood from dozens of cuts. She groped around until she found her four-year-old daughter Ikuko. She saw no trace of her husband. Dazed and terrified, she took the child's hand and fled.

But Michiyoshi Nukushina was there, and was still alive, though buried unconscious inside the wreckage of his home. His life had been saved because the blast blew him into a corner where two big, old-fashioned office safes, used in the family wine business, took the weight of the roof when it fell and thus spared him from being crushed. As he came to, raised his head and looked around, everything seemed strangely reddened. He discovered later that blood from cuts on his head had gushed down over his eyelids, forming a sort of red filter over his eyes. His first conscious thought was that the emergency water tank kept on hand for fire-bombing protection was only one-third full. As his head cleared, he called for his wife and daughter. There was no reply. Getting painfully to his feet—his left leg was badly broken—he found a stick for a crutch and hobbled out of the rubble.

Hold out your left hand, palm down, fingers spread, and you have a rough outline of the shape of Hiroshima. The sea is beyond the fingertips. The back of the hand is where the Ota River comes down from the hills to the north. The spot where the bomb exploded is about where a wedding ring would be worn, just south of the main military headquarters and in the center of the residential-commercial districts of the city. Major Ferebee's aim was nearly perfect. Little Boy was **detonated**[2] little more than two hundred yards from the aiming point on his target chart, despite the fact that it was released from a fast-moving aircraft over three miles to the east and nearly six miles up in the air.

Dropped with such precision, the bomb performed better than its makers had predicted. Several factors combined by chance to produce even more devastation than had been expected.

---

[2] **detonated**—set off, caused to explode.

First was the time of the explosion. All over Hiroshima, thousands of the charcoal **braziers**[3] that were the stoves in most households were still full of hot coals after being used for breakfast cooking. Almost every stove was knocked over by the massive blast wave that followed the explosion, and each became an **incendiary**[4] torch to set fire to the wood-and-paper houses. In addition, where [J. Robert] Oppenheimer had estimated casualties on the assumption that most people would be inside their air-raid shelters, almost no one in Hiroshima was sheltered when the bomb actually fell. The recent all-clear, the fact that it was a time when most people were on their way to work, the mischance by which there had been no new alert when the *Enola Gay* approached the city, the fact that small formations of planes had flown over many times before without dropping bombs, all combined to leave people exposed. Thus more than seventy thousand persons instead of Oppenheimer's estimate of twenty thousand were killed outright or so badly injured that they were dead in a matter of hours.

The initial flash spawned a succession of **calamities**.[5]

First came heat. It lasted only an instant but was so intense that it melted roof tiles, fused the quartz crystals in granite blocks, charred the exposed sides of telephone poles for almost two miles, and incinerated nearby humans so thoroughly that nothing remained except their shadows, burned into asphalt pavements or stone walls. Of course the heat was most intense near the "ground zero" point, but for thousands of yards it had the power to burn deeply. Bare skin was burned up to two and a half miles away.

A printed page was exposed to the heat rays a mile and a half from the point of explosion, and the black

---

[3] **braziers**—pans for holding burning coals, often used in cooking.

[4] **incendiary**—having the ability to set on fire.

[5] **calamities**—grave events marked by great loss and distress.

letters were burned right out of the white paper. Hundreds of women learned a more personal lesson in the varying heat-absorption qualities of different colors when darker parts of their clothing burned out while lighter shades remained unscorched, leaving skin underneath etched in precise detail with the flower patterns of their kimonos. A dress with blue polka dots printed on white material came out of the heat with dark dots completely gone but the white background barely singed. A similar phenomenon occurred in men's shirts. Dark stripes were burned out while the alternate light stripes were undamaged. Another factor that affected injury was the thickness of clothing. Many people had their skin burned except where a double-thickness seam or a folded lapel had stood between them and the fireball. Men wearing caps emerged with sharp lines etched across their temples. Below the line, exposed skin was burned, while above it, under the cap, there was no injury. Laborers working in the open with only undershirts on had the looping pattern of shoulder straps and armholes printed on their chests. Sometimes clothing protected the wearer only if it hung loosely. One man standing with his arm bent, so that the sleeve was drawn tightly over his elbow, was burned only around that joint.

The heat struck only what stood in the direct path of its straight-line radiation from the fireball. A man sitting at his desk writing a letter had his hands deeply burned because the heat rays coming through his window fell directly on them, while his face, only eighteen inches away but outside the path of the rays, was unmarked. In countless cases the human body was burned or spared by the peculiarity of its position at the moment of flash. A walking man whose arm was swinging forward at the critical instant was burned all down the side of his torso. Another, whose moving arm happened to be next to his body, was left with an unburned streak where the limb had blocked out the radiation. In scores of cases people were burned on one side of the face but not on the other because they had been standing or sitting in profile to the explosion. A shirtless laborer was burned all across his back—except for a narrow strip where the slight hollow down his spine left the skin in a "shadow" where the heat rays could not fall.

Some measure of the heat's intensity can be gained from the experience of the mayor of Kabe, a village ten miles outside the city. He was standing in his garden and even at that distance distinctly felt the heat on his face when the bomb exploded.

After the heat came the blast, sweeping outward from the fireball with the force of a five-hundred mile-an-hour wind. Only those objects that offered a minimum of surface resistance—handrails on bridges, pipes, utility poles—remained standing. The walls of a few office buildings, specially built to resist earthquakes, remained standing, but they now enclosed nothing but wreckage, as their roofs were driven down to the ground, carrying everything inside down under them. Otherwise, in a giant circle more than two miles across, everything was reduced to rubble. The blast drove all before it. The stone columns flanking the entrance to the Shima Surgical Hospital, directly underneath the explosion, were rammed straight down into the ground. Every hard object that was dislodged, every brick, every broken timber, every roof tile, became a potentially lethal missile. Every window in the city was suddenly a shower of sharp glass splinters, driven with such speed and force that in hundreds of buildings they were deeply imbedded in walls—or in people. Many people were picking tiny shards of glass from their eyes for weeks afterward as a result of the shattering of their spectacles, or trying to wash out bits of sand and grit driven under their eyelids.

Even a blade of grass now became a weapon to injure the man who tended it. A group of boys working in an open field had their backs peppered with bits of grass and straw which hit them with such force that they were driven into the flesh.

Many were struck down by a combination of the heat and the blast. A group of schoolgirls was working on the roof of a building, removing tiles as the structure was being demolished for a firebreak. Thus completely exposed, they were doubly hurt, burned and then blown to the ground. So quickly did the blast follow the heat that for many they seemed to come together. One man, knocked sprawling when the blast blew in his window, looked up from the floor to see a wood-and-paper screen across the room burning briskly.

Heat and blast together started and fed fires in thousands of places within a few seconds, thus instantly rendering useless the painfully constructed firebreaks. In some spots the ground itself seemed to spout fire, so numerous were the flickering little jets of flame spontaneously ignited by the radiant heat. The city's fire stations were crushed or burned along with everything else, and two-thirds of Hiroshima's firemen were killed or wounded. Even if it had been left intact, the fire department could have done little or nothing to save the city. Not only were there too many fires, but the blast had broken open the city's water mains in seventy thousand places, so there was no pressure. Between them, blast and fire destroyed every single building within an area of almost five square miles around the zero point. Although the walls of thirty structures still stood, they were no more than empty shells.

After heat, blast, and fire, the people of Hiroshima had still other ordeals ahead of them. A few minutes after the explosion, a strange rain began to fall. The raindrops were as big as marbles—and they were black. This frightening phenomenon resulted from the vaporization of moisture in the fireball and condensation in the cloud that spouted up from it. As the cloud, carrying water vapor and the pulverized dust of Hiroshima, reached colder air at higher altitudes, the moisture condensed and fell out as rain. There was not enough to put out the fires, but there was enough of this "black rain" to heighten the bewilderment and panic of people already unnerved by what had hit them.

After the rain came a wind—the great "fire wind"—which blew back in toward the center of the catastrophe, increasing in force as the air over Hiroshima grew hotter and hotter because of the great fires. The wind blew so hard that it uprooted huge trees in the parks where survivors were collecting. It whipped up high waves on the rivers of Hiroshima and drowned many who had gone into the water in an attempt to escape from the heat and flames around them. Some of those who drowned had been pushed into the rivers when the crush of fleeing people overflowed the bridges, making fatal bottlenecks of the only escape routes from the stricken islands. Thousands of people were simply fleeing, blindly and without an objective except to get out of the city. Some in the suburbs, seeing them come, thought at first they were Negroes, not Japanese, so blackened were their skins. The refugees could not explain what had burned them. "We saw the flash," they said, "and this is what happened."

One of those who struggled toward a bridge was Nukushina, the wine seller turned fireman whose life had been saved by the big office safes in his house just over a half mile from "zero," the point over which the bomb exploded. Leaning on his stick, he limped to the Sumiyoshi bridge a few hundred yards away, where, with unusual foresight, he kept a small boat tied up, loaded with fresh water and a little food, ready for any possible emergency.

"I found my boat intact," he recalled later, "but it was already filled with other desperate victims. As I stood on the bridge wondering what to do next, black drops of rain began to splatter down. The river itself and the river banks were teeming with horrible specimens of humans who had survived and come seeking safety to the river."

Fortunately for Nukushina, another boat came by, operated by a friend who offered to take him on board.

"With his assistance, I climbed into the boat. At that time, they pointed out to me that my intestines were dangling from my stomach but there was nothing I could do about it. My clothes, boots and everything were blown off my person, leaving me with only my loincloth. Survivors swimming in the river shouted for help, and as we leaned down to pull them aboard, the skin from their arms and hands literally peeled off into our hands.

"A fifteen- or sixteen-year-old girl suddenly popped up alongside our boat and as we offered her our hand to pull her on board, the front of her face suddenly dropped off as though it were a mask. The nose and other facial features suddenly dropped off with the mask, leaving only a pink, peachlike face front with holes where the eyes, nose and mouth used to be. As the head dropped under the surface, the girl's black hair left a swirling black eddy. . . ."

Here Nukushina mercifully lost consciousness. He came to five hours later as he was being transferred into a launch that carried him, with other wounded, to an emergency first-aid station set up on the island of Ninoshima in the harbor. There he found safety, but no medical care. Only twenty-eight doctors were left alive and able to work in a city of a quarter million people, fully half of whom were casualties.

When Hayano Susukida tried to get up off the ground onto which she and the other members of her tile-salvaging labor gang had been thrown, she thought she was going to die. Her whole back, bared by the blast, burned and stung when she moved. But the thought of her four-year-old daughter Kazuko, who had been evacuated from the city after Hayano's husband was sent overseas and the family home had been marked for destruction in the firebreak program, made her try again. This time she got to her feet and staggered home. The blast had not leveled her house, about a mile and a quarter from the zero point, and the fire had not yet reached it. Hurriedly she stuffed a few things—a bottle of vegetable oil, some mosquito netting, two quilts, a small radio—into an old baby carriage, and started wheeling it toward the nearest bomb shelter. After going a few feet, she had to carry the carriage, for the street was choked with debris. She reached the shelter and passed the oil around to those inside, using the last of it to salve her own burns, which had not blistered or peeled but were nevertheless strangely penetrating and painful. She wondered what time it was. Her wrist watch was gone, so she walked home again to get her alarm clock. It was still running; it showed a little after ten. Back at the shelter, she just sat and waited. At noon someone handed out a few rice balls. As the survivors ate, an Army truck miraculously appeared and carried them to the water front, just beyond the edge of the bomb's destruction. Then they were ferried over to the emergency hospital on Ninoshima Island.

Dr. Imagawa, a little further from the center of the blast, was not seriously injured, although he was cut by flying glass in a number of places. His first reaction was annoyance. His clothes were in tatters, and he wondered how he would find the new pair of shoes which he had left at his patient's front door. Helping the small boy down off the five-foot rubble pile that had been the sickroom, he asked the youngster to take him to the front door. Oddly enough, they could not even find where the front of the house had been. Imagawa, much to his disgust, was out a new pair of shoes. At an artesian well[6] with a pump that was still operating, he washed as best he could and set out for suburban Furue where his wife and children should be. He stopped frequently in response to appeals for help from the injured. One was a woman who wandered aimlessly in the street holding her bare breast, which had been split open. She pleaded with him to tell her whether she would live. The doctor, although positive she could not survive, assured her that a mere breast injury would not be fatal. Later, he drew water for a score of wounded from another well pump. Down the street, a trolley car burned briskly. Finally he got clear of the city and climbed the hill to Furue, where he found his family safe and uninjured. The walls of the house had cracked, in some places fallen, but his wife and the two little children had escaped injury, while the oldest girl had walked home from school without a scratch after the blast. The doctor ate, washed thoroughly, painted his cuts with **iodine**[7] and worked till dark with his wife cleaning up their house. That evening the somewhat **sybaritic**[8] physician sat down to dinner and then relaxed, as he had done the night before in Hiroshima—twenty-four hours and an age earlier—over a few cups of wine.

---

[6] artesian well—well in which the water is under pressure, especially one in which the water flows to the surface naturally.

[7] **iodine**—element used in medicine to clean wounds.

[8] **sybaritic**—luxury-loving; one who is interested in gratifying his appetites or senses.

The doctor sipping his wine that night had one thing in common with Mrs. Susukida and Michiyoshi Nukushina, both lying injured and untended in the emergency hospital on Ninoshima Island. None of them knew what it was that had destroyed their city. Nor did they yet have either time or inclination to wonder.

QUESTIONS TO CONSIDER

1. How would you describe the reaction of the survivors to what has happened? What seem to be their greatest concerns?

2. What was the black rain? How did it affect the survivors?

3. How is the heat generated by the atomic bomb unusual? How do Knebel and Bailey describe the heat caused by the blast?

4. How would you have reacted had you been in Hiroshima that day?

from

Hiroshima

BY JOHN HERSEY

John Hersey (1914–1993) was an American journalist and novelist. Hersey had worked extensively as a war correspondent and during the war published three books about the soldiers' experiences. In 1946, Hersey went to visit Hiroshima and wrote an account of the effect of the bombing on six survivors. Hersey presented a horrifying story in a neutral tone, allowing the facts to speak for themselves. His account made a huge public impact when it was published in The New Yorker *in 1946 and went on to became a best-selling book.*

At nearly midnight, the night before the bomb was dropped, an announcer on the city's radio station said that about two hundred B-29s were approaching southern Honshu and advised the population of Hiroshima to **evacuate**[1] to their designated "safe areas." Mrs. Hatsuyo Nakamura, the tailor's widow, who lived in the section

---

[1] **evacuate**—remove or leave, especially from a military zone or dangerous area.

called Nobori-cho and who had long had a habit of doing as she was told, got her three children—a ten-year-old boy, Toshio, an eight-year-old girl, Yaeko, and a five-year-old girl, Myeko—out of bed and dressed them and walked with them to the military area known as the East Parade Ground, on the northeast edge of the city. There she unrolled some mats and the children lay down on them. They slept until about two, when they were awakened by the roar of the planes going over Hiroshima.

As soon as the planes had passed, Mrs. Nakamura started back with her children. They reached home a little after two-thirty and she immediately turned on the radio, which, to her distress, was just then broadcasting a fresh warning. When she looked at the children and saw how tired they were, and when she thought of the number of trips they had made in past weeks, all to no purpose, to the East Parade Ground, she decided that in spite of the instructions on the radio, she simply could not face starting out all over again. She put the children in their bedrolls on the floor, lay down herself at three o'clock, and fell asleep at once, so soundly that when planes passed over later, she did not waken to their sound.

The siren jarred her awake at about seven. She arose, dressed quickly, and hurried to the house of Mr. Nakamoto, the head of her Neighborhood Association, and asked him what she should do. He said that she should remain at home unless an urgent warning—a series of **intermittent**[2] blasts of the siren—was sounded. She returned home, lit the stove in the kitchen, set some rice to cook, and sat down to read that morning's Hiroshima *Chugoku*. To her relief, the all-clear sounded at eight o'clock. She heard the children stirring, so she went and gave each of them a handful of peanuts and told them to stay on their bedrolls, because they were

---

[2] **intermittent**—stopping and beginning again.

tired from the night's walk. She had hoped that they would go back to sleep, but the man in the house directly to the south began to make a terrible **hullabaloo**[3] of hammering, wedging, ripping, and splitting. The prefectural government, convinced, as everyone in Hiroshima was, that the city would be attacked soon, had begun to press with threats and warnings for the completion of wide fire lanes, which, it was hoped, might act in conjunction with the rivers to localize any fires started by an incendiary raid; and the neighbor was reluctantly sacrificing his home to the city's safety. Just the day before, the **prefecture**[4] had ordered all able-bodied girls from the secondary schools to spend a few days helping to clear these lanes, and they started work soon after the all-clear sounded.

Mrs. Nakamura went back to the kitchen, looked at the rice, and began watching the man next door. At first, she was annoyed with him for making so much noise, but then she was moved almost to tears by pity. Her emotion was specifically directed toward her neighbor, tearing down his home, board by board, at a time when there was so much unavoidable destruction, but undoubtedly she also felt a generalized, community pity, to say nothing of self-pity. She had not had an easy time. Her husband, Isawa, had gone into the Army just after Myeko was born, and she had heard nothing from or of him for a long time, until, on March 5, 1942, she received a seven-word telegram: "Isawa died an honorable death at Singapore." She learned later that he had died on February 15th, the day Singapore fell, and that he had been a corporal. Isawa had been a not particularly **prosperous**[5] tailor, and his only capital was a Sankoku

---

[3] **hullabaloo**—loud noise or disturbance.

[4] **prefecture**—district or territory (like a county).

[5] **prosperous**—successful, well-to-do.

sewing machine. After his death, when his allotments stopped coming, Mrs. Nakamura got out the machine and began to take in piecework herself, and since then had supported the children, but poorly, by sewing.

As Mrs. Nakamura stood watching her neighbor, everything flashed whiter than any white she had ever seen. She did not notice what happened to the man next door; the reflex of a mother set her in motion toward her children. She had taken a single step (the house was 1,350 yards, or three-quarters of a mile, from the center of the explosion) when something picked her up and she seemed to fly into the next room over the raised sleeping platform, pursued by parts of her house.

Timbers fell around her as she landed, and a shower of tiles **pommelled**[6] her; everything became dark, for she was buried. The debris did not cover her deeply. She rose up and freed herself. She heard a child cry," Mother, help me!," and saw her youngest—Myeko, the five-year-old—buried up to her breast and unable to move. As Mrs. Nakamura started frantically to claw her way toward the baby, she could see or hear nothing of her other children.

---

[6] **pommelled**—pounded, beaten, struck.

QUESTIONS TO CONSIDER

1. Why do Mrs. Nakamura and her children go to the East Parade Ground?

2. What is ironic about the situation of the man next door to Mrs. Nakamura?

3. Do you think it would have been better for the United States to have dropped the atomic bomb during the night? Why or why not?

from

Children of the A-Bomb

BY DR. ARATA OSADA

Arata Osada was a doctor who treated many survivors of the Hiroshima bombing. His book Children of the A-Bomb *details the effect of the bombing on children by retelling their stories of the bombing and its effect on their lives.*

Wakako Washino
—8th grade girl. In 2nd grade in 1945.—

That atom bomb—even the memory of it is hateful. The time the atom bomb fell I was in second grade. The seventh year has already come since I was separated from my brother when I was so little.

Since my brother liked swimming he often used to take me swimming with him and he often played with me. It was because he got water in his ear and on the night of the 5th it began to hurt so he couldn't wait any longer and went to Hiroshima. On the morning of the 6th he took his own money that he'd been saving up and he got on the seven o'clock train, and that turned out to be 'Farewell.'

Mother, who didn't know that he had left, thought that he had gone to school and she wasn't worried about him. Just as Brother's train was due to arrive, there was a flash and immediately afterward a rumble, and at the same time a horrible cloud floated upward. The minute I saw the cloud the thought came to my head that Brother was on the train, and frantically I ran all the way back to the house. When I reached the house I saw that the paper doors had been blown out, the electric lights were broken and fragments of glass were lying around. Outside there was so much glass and stuff it was dangerous to go barefoot, and people were running around and shouting. Everything was in a state of complete confusion. This was just a month after my father had been killed in the war. Since there was no one to take the lead in going to search for Brother, Mother and I went to our relatives to ask them to go. My uncle and my cousin went in the truck to look for Brother. However, they weren't allowed to enter Hiroshima. Mother and I stood beside the highway and looked at the faces one by one of every person who came along. But they were all strangers and no one passed who even looked like Brother. Poor things, they were every one of them covered with burns and wounds. Little as I was, I bowed my head. For days and days after that we did nothing but look for Brother. We didn't even eat very much. But in the end we never did find him. We put Brother's photograph in a box and we had a funeral.

Brother had no idea himself that he was going to die and every day he would say, "When Father's ashes come back, I can go and get them, can't I, Mom?"

He was always asking and every day he was waiting like this for Daddy's ashes. It turned out that the one who was waiting to receive the ashes had his funeral first.

When I think that all these things happened because of war, I hate it so that I can't stand it. With every year that passes I yearn more and more for my father and my brother so that I can hardly bear it.

The time the atom bomb fell I was so little that I didn't really understand what it was all about, and I have written only the things that stayed strongly in my head. From this day on I think from the bottom of my heart that we ought to throw away such barbaric things as atomic bombs and choose the path of peace.

Yasushi Haraki
—8th grade boy. In 2nd grade in 1945.—

At the time, I was in second grade. On that day they had been saying, "Air raid! Air raid!" since early in the morning. Then the **precautionary**[1] and first all-clear sounded. So I went to school and Mother went out with the Labor Service Group. My little sister was left alone at home. At school I was doing my homework. That was about 8 o'clock.

Then suddenly there was a flash and it got dark and in that same instant the ceiling came falling down. I was pinned under it. I was able to get out by going under the desks. By the time I got outside, already the whole place was like a sea of flames. The school, too, was burning, fiercely. I went back toward home but my house was also burning fiercely. Since there is no help for it, I take off, running toward Hijiyama. However, since my foot hurt and I had a wound on my stomach, I finally couldn't walk anymore and I stopped beside a bridge. Here Mother just happened to come past. I was terribly happy. I had a cut on my stomach and Mother had some bad wounds too, so the two of us went to the hospital at Ujina and stayed there two weeks. On the way from Hijiyama to Ujina there were lots of corpses lying all over the place. After two weeks had passed we went to a temple in the country. And we stayed at the temple for a little while.

---

[1] **precautionary**—taking care in advance or beforehand.

Mother and I came to the country, but we didn't know where my little sister had gone so we came back to Hiroshima again. When we searched here and there we found her with some people we didn't know. We promptly thanked them and took her over. But since she had been pinned under the house and hurt her legs and breathed the poison, she died about an hour later. Since there was nothing we could do, we left her body at the Hijiyama temple and we went back to the Ujina Hospital. The next day we went to Hijiyama and we made an offering of water to my dead sister and came back to the hospital.

One morning when we went as usual to offer the water we found that my sister's corpse was gone. We were told that some people had **cremated**[2] it for us together with their own dead. But we did not know who had cremated it for us and we were not able to recover the ashes. However there was no help for it so we went back to where our own house had been and dug around there. We found some bones although we did not know whose bones they were. Again there was no help for it. So we took those bones and returned to the country.

More than a month of days flowed past after the day of the A-bomb. My mother's younger sister and all of our relatives died. The only ones who were left alive were: I and Mother. Then we left the countryside and came back to Hiroshima.

When we arrived in Hiroshima there were temporary buildings standing here and there. The two of us went to Ujina and I attended the Ujina Grammar School and Mother worked in a restaurant. The war ended and lots of soldiers returned to the port of Ujina and they came to that restaurant.

One day I returned from school and was playing. On that day too, lots of soldiers came and were eating

---

[2] **cremated**—reduced to ashes by burning.

this and that. Suddenly when I looked at one of the soldiers I had a feeling that I had seen him somewhere. Only where I'd seen him I couldn't remember, so I didn't say anything. That soldier went away. Then after several days someone came asking for us. It was this same man. But I didn't know who it was so I just kept quiet and listened. Finally I understood that he was my own father.

Mother was terribly happy. Since Father had come back from the war, we moved. And then just as I thought our family had settled down our father got sick because at the war he had to eat weeds and things. And then a short two and a half months later he died. When my father died I was in third grade.

After Father died, Mother and I went back to the country. My father died and my little sister died and it was a terribly sad thing. After this Mother worked again for my sake. I was attending school in the country.

When I finished sixth grade we again went to Hiroshima, for family reasons.

Now we are in Nakata and the days and months of six years have flowed away since the dropping of the atom bomb. I think we ought to give up the ideas we have had up to now—give up the idea of war and try to make a good Japan.

Takako Okimoto
—8th grade girl. In 2nd grade in 1945.—

The 6th of August 1945—which I do not forget—the things that happened this day are deeply carved in my heart. That cruel war that snatched away so many precious human lives in one second—even now I shudder when I think of it. I am all alone after losing my father and mother and all my brothers and sisters. And no one can take their place. All of them, as a result of that A-bomb, were struck down one after another. My oldest brother was never found after he left to work with the Labor Service Group. My second brother's whole body was covered with burns and he died the next day at the Koi Grammar School. We left his body there at the Koi school and Father and Mother and the rest of us returned to the country. Since there were no good doctors in the country, my mother returned to town for treatment. At night a man came saying that she had become suddenly worse and called us back to town. My father and my little sister and I took the first morning train to town. When we arrived a strange, bad odor was rising everywhere, and the sights we saw! Everything imaginable was in ruins. You could not see a trace of the former Hiroshima. When we somehow managed to reach home we found that Mother had breathed her last a few minutes before. I cried for all I was worth. We cremated Mother's corpse on the stony river bed. Here and there all along the shore people were cremating corpses. And that evening just after we arrived back at my uncle's house in the country with Mother's ashes, my big sister died. Because I was still so little I didn't know what I ought to do but I put all my energy into nursing the father and sister who were left to me. But my little sister who was so cute died the day after my big sister's funeral. Father was able to go to my big sister's funeral but he no longer had any strength to get up for my little sister's funeral. I wonder whether the priest who came for my sister's funerals had also breathed the poison? He was no longer around at the time of Father's funeral.

As they all died like this one after another, there is no doubt that my father who lasted the longest must have lost all hope.

But even so when I asked him, "Father, how are you this morning?" Father always answered to keep my spirits up, "This morning I feel a little better."

The fact was, his bodily health kept getting only worse. Full of anxiety over me because he was leaving me all alone, Father departed from this world.

Before he died Father often said, "Father doesn't want to die. Since our house and our clothes have all been burned by the A-bomb, let's both of us go in our rags to the country and be farmers." He said this often.

On the 15th of August Japan finally became a defeated country. Many beggars appeared in front of the station, and thieves and armed bandits have turned up one after the other, and it has become a world where you aren't safe for a minute.

What has caused this sort of thing? It is because of war. If there were no wars such miserable people would never appear and the world would always be a place of peace. In the new Constitution, **renunciation**[3] of war is determined. Even if it isn't a case of war between one country and another, even inside the country of Japan, in spite of the fact that we are the same kind of people, there is always war going on. As long as this is the case we will not become a peaceful country. In order to build a peaceful country, I believe we must first be considerate of each other.

---

[3] **renunciation**—the formal act of giving up or refusing.

QUESTIONS TO CONSIDER

1. How would you describe the tone of these children's stories?

2. What do most of the survivors seem concerned with?

3. How did the atomic bomb affect these children's attitude toward war?

Interview of an A-Bomb Survivor: Ms. Michiko Yamaoka

INTERVIEW BY MITSURU OHBA

The Atomic Bomb website in Japan features a great deal of fascinating information, among it interviews like the one below with survivors. What follows here is a first-person account years later with a survivor at the Peace Memorial in Hiroshima.

date: June 4, 1995
place: Lobby, Peace Memorial Museum
interviewer: Mitsuru Ohba

Ms. Yamaoka is one of the volunteers who talks about her experiences with the A-bomb to people who visit Hiroshima. She was a middle school student when the bomb was dropped. She was one of the 25 girls who were invited to New York in 1955 for operations by an American organization, Friends, and stayed there for one and a half years. After her return from New York, she opened a dress-making school for young women to help her mother who had been suffering from the side effects of the bomb. She did not talk about the bomb for the first thirty years. After the death of her mother, she volunteered to talk about her experiences to young Japanese; this is now her life work. She has visited the U.S. twice in the last 20 years to tell her story.

1. Where were you at the time the bomb was dropped?

I was walking on the street. Two of my cousins and I had left home only a few minutes before that. I was heading West; they were heading East. I was a half mile away from the center of the explosion. I heard the sound of a B-29 bomber. I was wondering why the bomber was flying over Hiroshima, as the military headquarters had not issued an alert.

2. What happened to you when the explosion occurred?

When I saw a very strong light, a flash, I put my arms over my face unconsciously. Almost instantly I felt my face was inflating. I thought I was directly hit by the bomb and was dying. I was proud of myself for dying for my country because we had been educated so. Shortly after, I felt my body flying in the air and then I lost consciousness.

3. What did you see when you regained consciousness?

I do not know how long I was unconscious. When I came to, I was in the dark. I was under a stack of broken bricks. I could not move. I heard voices asking for help or asking for water. I understood that something special must have happened to us. I was in the dark for some time. I heard something burning near me. I do not know how long I was there; it could have been half an hour, it could have been several hours. Suddenly I heard my mother's voice calling my name. I called my mother. I heard someone saying to my mother "It's too dangerous; it's impossible." My mother still called my name and I called to my mother. She was trying to rescue me from the fire. Shortly after she found and rescued me.

4. What did you see after that?

When I was rescued, my hair was burned; my face was inflated like a balloon. Though my mother did not say, I knew it. I wondered why my shirt had been burnt and hanging around my arms, I soon realized they were pieces of my skin. It was hell. I saw people looking for water and they died soon after they drank it. I saw many people go to the river in search of water and who died. The whole city was destroyed and burning. There was no place to go. My mother told me to leave Hiroshima and to stay at my cousins' house in the countryside. I stayed there for a year and then came back to Hiroshima. I wanted to see my mother again before I died. My two cousins were lost and were never found. When I returned, Hiroshima was still a destroyed city.

5. What was the major physical effect of the bomb?

Though many people say that they felt the heat, I did not. I did not feel the wind either. I think I was too close to the center of the explosion to feel the heat and the wind. My skin was badly burned. I felt my body flying in the air. That was it.

6. How was your stay in New York? What did you feel?

I was thinking only of my complete recovery. I was young. I thought that it was their duty to help me because they had dropped the bomb and hurt us. I had many operations over one and a half years. Seven different families hosted me. I did not know they were volunteers. I found out that there was no official financial support for the project. The project was supported by the good-will of many American citizens. Now I really appreciate that.

7. What do you want to tell the world?

Though the U.S. government wanted to **terminate**[1] the war quickly, the country is responsible for the results of the decision. Every country is responsible for its decision to develop, possess and use nuclear weapons, or weapons of total destruction. If we really know what they are, we can understand that we should never **duplicate**[2] the failure. It should never happen again. It is really important to know the facts about the A-bomb. I hope as many children in the world as possible know what happened in Hiroshima and Nagasaki, and learn what weapons of total destruction can mean to human beings.

---

[1] **terminate**—end, stop.
[2] **duplicate**—repeat.

QUESTIONS TO CONSIDER

1. Why do you think Ms. Yamaoka survived when her two cousins did not?

2. Why does Ms. Yamaoka make a good ambassador for peace?

3. What do you find most persuasive about her appeal to stop the use of atomic weapons?

Atomic Bombing of Nagasaki

BY WILLIAM L. LAURENCE

William L. Laurence was the chief science reporter of The New York Times *during World War II. In the summer of 1945, he was chosen to be the only journalist covering the top secret project building the first atomic bombs. Laurence was able to immerse himself in the project. He saw the Trinity test in July, was at Tinian when the* Enola Gay *left to drop the first bomb on Hiroshima, and was able to fly on the mission that dropped the bomb on Nagasaki. His story describing this event, excerpted below, appeared two months after the bombing.*

With the atomic bomb mission to Japan, Aug. 9 (Delayed)—We are on our way to bomb the mainland of Japan. Our flying contingent consists of three specially designed B-29 "Superforts," and two of these carry no bombs. But our plane is on its way with another atomic bomb, the second in three days, concentrating in its active substance an explosive energy equivalent to 20,000 and, under favorable conditions, 40,000 tons of TNT.

We have several chosen targets. One of these is the great industrial and shipping center of Nagasaki, on the western shore of Kyushu, one of the main islands of the Japanese homeland.

I watched the assembly of this man-made **meteor**[1] during the past two days, and was among the small group of scientists and Army and Navy representatives privileged to be present at the ritual of its loading in the "Superfort" last night, against a background of threatening black skies torn open at intervals by great lightning flashes.

It is a thing of beauty to behold, this "gadget." In its design went millions of man-hours of what is without doubt the most concentrated intellectual effort in history. Never before had so much brain-power been focused on a single problem.

This atomic bomb is different from the bomb used three days ago with such devastating results on Hiroshima.

I saw the atomic substance before it was placed inside the bomb. By itself it is not at all dangerous to handle. It is only under certain conditions, produced in the bomb assembly, that it can be made to yield up its energy, and even then it gives only a small fraction of its total contents—a fraction, however, large enough to produce the greatest explosion on earth.

The briefing at midnight revealed the extreme care and the tremendous amount of preparation that had been made to take care of every detail of the mission, to make certain that the atomic bomb fully served the purpose for which it was intended. Each target in turn was shown in detailed maps and in aerial photographs. Every detail of the course was rehearsed—navigation, altitude, weather, where to land in emergencies. It came out that the Navy had submarines and rescue craft,

---

[1] **meteor**—mass of stone or metal, bomb.

known as Dumbos and Superdumbos, stationed at various strategic points in the vicinity of the targets, ready to rescue the fliers in case they were forced to bail out.

The briefing period ended with a moving prayer by the **chaplain**.[2] We then proceeded to the mess hall for the traditional early morning breakfast before departure on a bombing mission.

A **convoy**[3] of trucks took us to the supply building for the special equipment carried on combat missions. This included the "Mae West," a parachute, a lifeboat, an oxygen mask, a flak suit and a survival vest. We still had a few hours before take-off time, but we all went to the flying field and stood around in little groups or sat in jeeps talking rather casually about our mission to the Empire, as the Japanese home islands are known hereabouts. . . .

We took off at 3:50 this morning and headed northwest on a straight line for the Empire. The night was cloudy and threatening, with only a few stars here and there breaking through the overcast. The weather report had predicted storms ahead part of the way but clear sailing for the final and climactic stages of our **odyssey**.[4]

We were about an hour away from our base when the storm broke. Our great ship took some heavy dips through the abysmal darkness around us but it took these dips much more gracefully than a large commercial airliner, producing a sensation more in the nature of a glide than a "bump," like a great ocean liner riding the waves, except that in this case the air waves were much higher and the rhythmic tempo of the glide much faster.

I noticed a strange eerie light coming through the window high above the navigator's cabin and as I peered through the dark all around us I saw a startling

---

[2] **chaplain**—clergyman or person who leads religious services.

[3] **convoy**—escort that protects.

[4] **odyssey**—long journey or voyage.

phenomenon. The whirling giant propellers had some-how became great **luminous**[5] disks of blue flame. The same luminous blue flame appeared on the plexiglass[6] windows in the nose of the ship, and on the tips of the giant wings—it looked as though we were riding the whirlwind through space on a chariot of blue fire.

It was, I surmised, a surcharge of static electricity that had accumulated on the tips of the propellers and on the dielectric material in the plastic windows. One's thoughts dwelt anxiously on the precious cargo in the invisible ship ahead of us. Was there any likelihood of danger that this heavy electric tension in the atmos-phere all about us might set it off?

I expressed my fears to Captain Bock, who seems **nonchalant**[7] and **imperturbed**[8] at the controls. He quickly reassures me:

"It is a familiar phenomenon seen often on ships. I have seen it many times on bombing missions. It is known as St. Elmo's Fire."

On we went through the night. We soon rode out the storm and our ship was once again sailing on a smooth course straight ahead, on a direct line to the Empire.

Our altimeter[9] showed that we were traveling through space at a height of 17,000 feet. The thermometer registered an outside temperature of 33 degrees below zero centigrade, about 30 below Fahrenheit. Inside our pressurized cabin the temperature was that of a comfort-able air-conditioned room, and a pressure corresponding to an altitude of 8,000 feet. Captain Bock cautioned me, however, to keep my oxygen mask handy in case of emergency. This, he explained, might mean either

---

[5] **luminous**—shining by its own light, like the sun or stars.

[6] plexiglass—light, clear plastic material used in place of glass because of its lightness and greater strength.

[7] **nonchalant**—appearing not to care, without interest or enthusiasm.

[8] **imperturbed**—calm.

[9] altimeter—a device for measuring altitude or how high a plane is flying.

something going wrong with the pressure equipment inside the ship or a hole through the cabin by flak.

The first signs of dawn came shortly after 5 o'clock. Sergeant Curry, who had been listening steadily on his earphones for radio reports, while maintaining a strict radio silence himself, greeted it by rising to his feet and gazing out the window.

"It's good to see the day," he told me. "I get a feeling of **claustrophobia**[10] hemmed in in this cabin at night."

He is a typical American youth, looking even younger than his 20 years. It takes no mind-reader to read his thoughts.

"It's a long way from Hoopeston, Ill.," I find myself remarking.

"Yep," he replies, as he busies himself decoding a message from outer space.

"Think this atomic bomb will end the war?" he asks hopefully.

"There is a very good chance that this one may do the trick," I assure him, "but if not, then the next one or two surely will. Its power is such that no nation can stand up against it very long."

This was not my own view. I had heard it expressed all around a few hours earlier, before we took off. To anyone who had seen this man-made fireball in action, as I had less than a month ago in the desert of New Mexico, this view did not sound overoptimistic.

By 5:50 it was real light outside. We had lost our lead ship, but Lieutenant Godfrey, our navigator, informs me that we had arranged for that **contingency**.[11] We have an assembly point in the sky above the little island of Yakoshima, southeast of Kyushu, at 9:10. We are to circle there and wait for the rest of our formation.

---

[10] **claustrophobia**—a fear of small, cramped rooms or places.

[11] **contingency**—depending on chance or an accident, not planned.

Our genial bombardier, Lieutenant Levy, comes over to invite me to take his front-row seat in the transparent nose of the ship and I accept eagerly. From that vantage point in space, 17,000 feet above the Pacific, one gets a view of hundreds of miles on all sides, horizontally and vertically. At that height the vast ocean below and the sky above seem to merge into one great sphere.

I was on the inside of that firmament, riding above the giant mountains of white **cumulous**[12] clouds, letting myself be suspended in infinite space. One hears the whirl of the motors behind one, but it soon becomes insignificant against the immensity all around and is before long swallowed by it. There comes a point where space also swallows time and one lives through eternal moments filled with an oppressive loneliness, as though all life had suddenly vanished from the earth and you are the only one left, a lone survivor traveling endlessly through **interplanetary**[13] space.

My mind soon returns to the mission I am on. Somewhere beyond these vast mountains of white clouds ahead of me there lies Japan, the land of our enemy. In about four hours from now one of its cities, making weapons of war for use against us, will be wiped off the map by the greatest weapon ever made by man. In one-tenth of a millionth of a second, a fraction of time immeasurable by any clock, a whirlwind from the skies will **pulverize**[14] thousands of its buildings and tens of thousands of its inhabitants.

Our weather planes ahead of us are on their way to find out where the wind blows. Half an hour before target time we will know what the winds have decided.

---

[12] **cumulous**—clouds with rounded heaps, often a sign of fair weather.

[13] **interplanetary**—between planets.

[14] **pulverize**—grind into dust or powder.

Does one feel any pity or compassion for the poor devils about to die? Not when one thinks of Pearl Harbor and of the Death March on Bataan.

Captain Bock informs me that we are about to start our climb to bombing altitude.

He manipulates a few knobs on his control panel to the right of him and I alternately watch the white clouds and ocean below me and the altimeter on the bombardier's panel. We reached our altitude at 9 o'clock. We were then over Japanese waters, close to their mainland. Lieutenant Godfrey motioned to me to look through his radar scope. Before me was the outline of our assembly point. We shall soon meet our lead ship and proceed to the final stage of our journey.

We reached Yakoshima at 9:12 and there, about 4,000 feet ahead of us, was The Great Artiste[15] with its precious load. I saw Lieutenant Godfrey and Sergeant Curry strap on their parachutes and I decided to do likewise.

We started circling. We saw little towns on the coastline, heedless of our presence. We kept on circling, waiting for the third ship in our formation.

It was 9:56 when we began heading for the coastline. Our weather scouts had sent us code messages, deciphered by Sergeant Curry, informing us that both the primary target as well as the secondary were clearly visible.

The winds of destiny seemed to favor certain Japanese cities that must remain nameless. We circled about them again and again and found no opening in the thick umbrella of clouds that covered them. Destiny chose Nagasaki as the ultimate target.

We had been circling for some time when we noticed black puffs of smoke coming through the white clouds directly at us. There were fifteen bursts of flak[16]

---

[15] The Great Artiste—name of the plane that dropped the atomic bomb on Nagasaki.

[16] flak—gunfire from an anti-aircraft cannon.

in rapid succession, all too low. Captain Bock changed his course. There soon followed eight more bursts of flak, right up to our altitude, but by this time were too far to the left.

We flew southward down the channel and at 11:33 crossed the coastline and headed straight for Nagasaki about 100 miles to the west. Here again we circled until we found an opening in the clouds. It was 12:01 and the goal of our mission had arrived.

We heard the prearranged signal on our radio, put on our arc-welder's glasses and watched tensely the maneuverings of the strike ship about half a mile in front of us.

"There she goes!" someone said.

Out of the belly of The Great Artiste what looked like a black object went downward.

Captain Bock swung around to get out of range; but even though we were turning away in the opposite direction, and despite the fact that it was broad daylight in our cabin, all of us became aware of a giant flash that broke through the dark barrier of our arc-welder's lenses and flooded our cabin with intense light.

We removed our glasses after the first flash, but the light still lingered on, a bluish-green light that illuminated the entire sky all around. A tremendous blast wave struck our ship and made it tremble from nose to tail. This was followed by four more blasts in rapid succession, each resounding like the boom of cannon fire hitting our plane from all directions.

Observers in the tail of our ship saw a giant ball of fire rise as though from the bowels of the earth, belching forth enormous white smoke rings. Next they saw a giant pillar of purple fire, 10,000 feet high, shooting skyward with enormous speed.

By the time our ship had made another turn in the direction of the atomic explosion the pillar of purple fire had reached the level of our altitude. Only about forty-five seconds had passed. Awe-struck, we watched it shoot upward like a meteor coming from the earth instead of from outer space, becoming ever more alive as it climbed skyward through the white clouds. It was no longer smoke, or dust, or even a cloud of fire. It was a living thing, a new species of being, born right before our incredulous eyes.

At one stage of its evolution, covering millions of years in terms of seconds, the entity assumed the form of a giant square totem pole, with its base about three miles long, tapering off to about a mile at the top. Its bottom was brown, its center was amber, its top white. But it was a living totem pole, carved with many grotesque masks grimacing at the earth.

Then, just when it appeared as though the thing has settled down into a state of permanence, there came shooting out of the top a giant mushroom that increased the height of the pillar to a total of 45,000 feet. The mushroom top was even more alive than the pillar, seething and boiling in a white fury of creamy foam, sizzling upward and then descending earthward, a thousand Old Faithful geysers rolled into one.

It kept struggling in an elemental fury, like a creature in the act of breaking the bonds that held it down. In a few seconds it had freed itself from its gigantic stem and floated upward with tremendous speed, its momentum carrying into the **stratosphere**[17] to a height of about 60,000 feet.

But no sooner did this happen when another mushroom, smaller in size than the first one, began emerging out of the pillar. It was as though the **decapitated**[18] monster was growing a new head.

---

[17] **stratosphere**—the upper part of the Earth's atmosphere, between 5 to 10 miles above the Earth.

[18] **decapitated**—having a head cut off.

As the first mushroom floated off into the blue it changed its shape into a flowerlike form, its giant petal curving downward, creamy white outside, rose-colored inside. It still retained that shape when we last gazed at it from a distance of about 200 miles.

The New York Times, September 9, 1945

QUESTIONS TO CONSIDER

1. What details does Laurence give at the beginning that let the reader know this is not just an ordinary mission?

2. What details, if any, most surprised you? Why?

3. If you were a reporter, would you have wanted to go on such an important and history-making mission? Why or why not?

Hiroshima

Ruined City The first atomic bomb destroyed the city of Hiroshima in seconds. At one moment, a city was flourishing, and in the next it was reduced to rubble.

Wasteland People who survived the blast report that very few buildings remained standing. The view below was taken from the Red Cross Hospital approximately one mile from the center of the bomb blast.

Victims Estimates of the death toll ranged from 70,000 to 80,000 people. But over the years the number of fatalities has risen far higher because so many people continued to die from radiation poisoning and burns. Immediately after the bombing, people took shelter wherever they could find it. Here victims are huddled in the bombed-out shell of a building.

▲

Suffering The suffering brought on by the blast was beyond
comprehension. Here a nurse's aid and a mother tend to a victim
in a makeshift hospital in a bank building.

▲

Memorial Services Here Japanese women attend Shinto services for blast victims.

Homeless Because of the widespread devastation, people were homeless and without shelter. The city fell into a state of chaos, and people fended for themselves as best they could. ▶

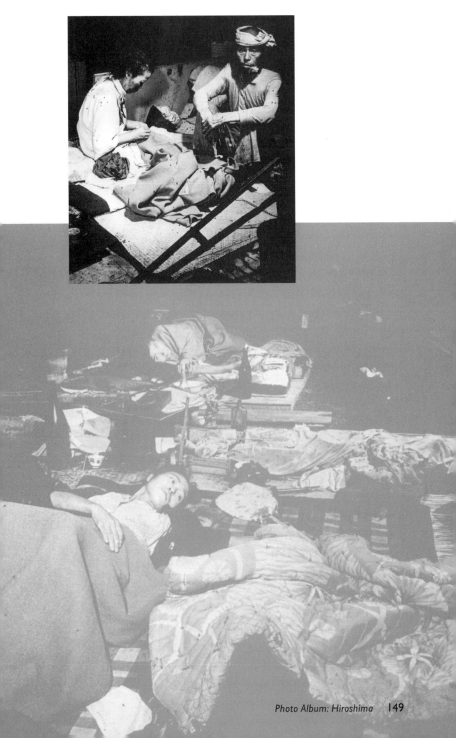

The Historical Debate

Hiroshima: Historians Reassess

BY GAR ALPEROVITZ

Gar Alperovitz is the leading figure among a group of historians who have been revising America's view of the use of the atomic bombs. His books Atomic Diplomacy: Hiroshima and Potsdam *(1965) and* The Decision to Use the Atomic Bomb *(1995) have put forth the thesis that the United States did not need to use the atomic bomb to end the war with Japan, which was on the verge of surrender. Instead, the atomic bomb was used to impress American strength on the Soviet Union and hence the first act of the Cold War. Alperovitz first developed his thesis in an article in* Foreign Policy *magazine in 1995.*

Earlier this year, the nation witnessed a massive media explosion surrounding the Smithsonian Institution's planned Enola Gay exhibit. As the 50th anniversary of the August 6, 1945, atomic bombing of Hiroshima approaches, Americans are about to receive another newspaper and television barrage.

Any serious attempt to understand the depth of feeling the story of the atomic bomb still arouses must confront two critical realities. First, there is a rapidly expanding gap between what the expert scholarly community now knows and what the public has been taught. Second, a steady narrowing of the questions in dispute in the most sophisticated studies has sharpened some of the truly controversial issues in the historical debate.

Consider the following assessment:

> Careful scholarly treatment of the records and manuscripts opened over the past few years has greatly enhanced our understanding of why the Truman administration used atomic weapons against Japan. Experts continue to disagree on some issues, but critical questions have been answered. The consensus among scholars is that the bomb was not needed to avoid an invasion of Japan and to end the war within a relatively short time. *It is clear that alternatives to the bomb existed and that Truman and his advisers knew it.* [Emphasis added.]

The author of that statement is not a revisionist; he is J. Samuel Walker, chief historian of the U.S. Nuclear Regulatory Commission. Nor is he alone in that opinion. Walker is summarizing the findings of modern specialists in his literature review in the Winter 1990 issue of *Diplomatic History*. Another expert review, by University of Illinois historian Robert Messer, concludes that recently discovered documents have been "devastating" to the traditional idea that using the bomb was the only way to avoid an invasion of Japan that might have cost many more lives.

Even allowing for continuing areas of dispute, these judgments are so far from the conventional wisdom that there is obviously something strange going on. One source of the divide between expert research and public understanding stems from a common feature of all serious scholarship: As in many areas of specialized research, perhaps a dozen truly knowledgeable experts are at the forefront of modern studies of the decision to use the atomic bomb. A second circle of generalists—historians concerned, for instance, with the Truman administration, with World War II in general, or even with the history of air power—depends heavily on the archival digging and analysis of the first circle. Beyond this second group are authors of general textbooks and articles and, still further out, journalists and other popular writers.

One can, of course, find many historians who still believe that the atomic bomb was needed to avoid an invasion. Among the inner circle of experts, however, conclusions that are at odds with this official rationale have long been commonplace. Indeed, as early as 1946 the U.S. Strategic Bombing Survey, in its report *Japan's Struggle to End the War*, concluded that "certainly prior to 31 December 1945, and in all probability prior to 1 November 1945, Japan would have surrendered even if the atomic bombs had not been dropped, even if Russia had not entered the war, and even if no invasion had been planned or contemplated."

Similarly, a top-secret April 1946 War Department Study, *Use of Atomic Bomb on Japan*, declassified during the 1970s but brought to broad public attention only in 1989, found that "the Japanese leaders had decided to surrender and were merely looking for sufficient **pretext**[1] to convince the die-hard Army Group that Japan had lost the war and must capitulate to the Allies." This official document judged that Russia's early-August entry into the war "would almost certainly have

---

[1] **pretext**—a false reason used in place of the real reason.

furnished this pretext, and would have been sufficient to convince all responsible leaders that surrender was unavoidable." The Study concluded that even an initial November 1945 landing on the southern Japanese island of Kyushu would have been only a "remote" possibility and that the full invasion of Japan in the spring of 1946 would not have occurred.

Military specialists who have examined Japanese decision-making have added to expert understanding that the bombing was unnecessary. For instance, political scientist Robert Pape's study, "Why Japan Surrendered," which appeared in the Fall 1993 issue of *International Security*, details Japan's military vulnerability, particularly its shortages of everything from ammunition and fuel to trained personnel: "Japan's military position was so poor that its leaders would likely have surrendered before invasion, and at roughly the same time in August 1945, even if the United States had not employed strategic bombing or the atomic bomb." In this situation, Pape stresses, "The Soviet invasion of Manchuria on August 9 raised Japan's military vulnerability to a very high level. The Soviet offensive ruptured Japanese lines immediately, and rapidly penetrated deep into the rear. Since the Kwantung Army was thought to be Japan's premier fighting force, this had a devastating effect on Japanese calculations of the prospects for home island defense." Pape adds, "If their best forces were so easily sliced to pieces, the unavoidable implication was that the less well-equipped and trained forces assembled for [the last decisive home island battle] had no chance of success against American forces that were even more capable than the Soviets."

Whether the use of the atomic bomb was in fact necessary is, of course, a different question from whether it was believed to be necessary at the time. Walker's summary of the expert literature is important because it underscores the availability of the alternatives to using the bomb, and because it documents that "Truman and his advisers knew" of the alternatives.

Several major strands of evidence have pushed many specialists in the direction of this startling conclusion. The United States had long since broken the enemy codes, and the president was informed of all important Japanese cable traffic. A critical message of July 12, 1945—just before Potsdam—showed that the Japanese emperor himself had decided to intervene to attempt to end the war. In his private journal, Truman bluntly characterized this message as the "telegram from [the] Jap Emperor asking for peace."

Other intercepted messages suggested that the main obstacle to peace was the continued Allied demand for unconditional surrender. Although the expert literature once mainly suggested that only one administration official—Undersecretary of State Joseph Grew—urged a change in the surrender formula to provide assurances for Japan's emperor, it is now clear that with the exception of Secretary of State James Byrnes, the entire top **echelon**[2] of the U.S. government advocated such a change. By June 1945, in fact, Franklin Roosevelt's secretary of state, Edward Stettinius (who remained in office until July 3); the undersecretary of state; the secretary of war; the secretary of the navy; the president's chief of staff, Admiral William Leahy; and Army Chief of Staff General George Marshall—plus all the members of the Joint Chiefs of Staff (JCS)—had in one way or another urged a clarification of the surrender formula. So, too, had the British military and civilian leadership, including Prime Minister Winston Churchill. Along with Grew, the joint Chiefs in particular recommended that a statement be issued to coincide with the fall of Okinawa, on or around June 21.

---

[2] **echelon**—level of command or authority.

At that time, war crimes trials were about to begin in Germany; the idea that the emperor might be hanged was a possibility Tokyo could not ignore. Because the Japanese regarded the emperor as a deity—more like Jesus or the Buddha than an ordinary human being—most top American officials deemed offering some assurances for the continuance of the dynasty an absolute necessity. The Joint Staff Planners, for instance, advised the Joint Chiefs in an April 25, 1945, report that "unless a definition of unconditional surrender can be given which is acceptable to the Japanese, there is no alternative to annihilation and no prospect that the threat of absolute defeat will bring about **capitulation**."[3]

Secretary of War Henry Stimson took essentially the same position in a July 2 memorandum to Truman. Moreover, he offered his assessment that a surrender formula could be acceptable to the Japanese, and stated "I think the Japanese nation has the mental intelligence and versatile capacity in such a crisis to recognize the folly of a fight to the finish and to accept the proffer of what will amount to an unconditional surrender."

As University of Southern Mississippi military historian John Ray Skates has noted in his book, *The Invasion of Japan: Alternative to the Bomb*, "[General] Marshall, who believed that retention [of the emperor] was a military necessity, asked that the members [of the Joint Chiefs of Staff] draft a memorandum to the president recommending that the Allies 'do nothing to indicate that the emperor might be removed from office upon unconditional surrender.'"

The other option that seemed likely to bring an end to the fighting concerned the Soviets. Joseph Stalin had promised to enter the war against Japan roughly three months after the May 8 defeat of Germany, which put the target date on or around August 8. Earlier in the

---

[3] **capitulation**—surrender under certain terms or circumstances.

war, the United States had sought Russia's help primarily to pin down Japanese armies in Manchuria and thus make a U.S. invasion of the home islands easier. By midsummer, however, Japan's position had deteriorated so much that top U.S. military planners believed the mere shock of a Red Army attack might be sufficient to bring about surrender and thus make an invasion unnecessary.

As early as February 1955, Harvard historian Ernest May, in an article in *Pacific Historical Review*, observed that the "Japanese diehards . . . had acknowledged since 1941 that Japan could not fight Russia as well as the United States and Britain." May also observed that because Moscow had been an outlet for various Japanese peace feelers, when the Soviet declaration of war finally occurred it "discouraged Japanese hopes of secretly negotiating terms of peace." Moreover, in the end, "The Emperor's appeal [to end the war] probably resulted, therefore, from the Russian action, but it could not, in any event, have been long in coming."

The importance to U.S. leaders of the "Russian shock option" for ending the war—which was widely discussed even in the 1945 press—disappeared from most scholarly studies during the Cold War. We now know, however, that as of April 29, 1945, the Joint Intelligence Committee (JIC), in a report titled *Unconditional Surrender of Japan*, informed the JCS that increasing "numbers of informed Japanese, both military and civilian, already realize the inevitability of absolute defeat." The JIC further advised that "the increasing effects of air-sea blockade, the progressive and **cumulative**[4] devastation wrought by strategic bombing, and the collapse of Germany (with its implications regarding redeployment) should make this realization widespread within the year."

---

[4] **cumulative**—increasing or growing in amount or force.

The JIC pointed out, however, that a Soviet decision to join with the United States and Great Britain would have enormous force and would dramatically alter the equation: "The entry of the USSR into the war would, together with the foregoing factors, convince most Japanese *at once* of the inevitability of complete defeat." [Emphasis added.]

By mid-June, Marshall advised Truman directly that "the impact of Russian entry [into the war] on the already hopeless Japanese may well be the decisive action levering them into capitulation at the time or shortly thereafter if we land in Japan." Again, Marshall's advice to Truman came almost a month before news of the emperor's personal intervention was received and four and a half months before even a preliminary Kyushu landing was to take place.

In July, the British general Sir Hastings Ismay, chief of staff to the minister of defence, summarized the conclusions of the latest U.S.–U.K. intelligence studies for Churchill in this way: "When Russia came into the war against Japan, the Japanese would probably wish to get out on almost any terms short of the dethronement of the Emperor."

On several occasions, Truman made abundantly clear that the main reason he went to Potsdam to meet Stalin was to make sure the Soviets would, in fact, enter the war. The atomic bomb had not yet been tested, and, as Truman later stated in his memoirs, "If the test [of the atomic bomb] should fail, then it would be even more important to us to bring about a surrender before we had to make a physical conquest of Japan."

Some of the most important modern documentary discoveries relate to this point. After Stalin confirmed that the Red Army would indeed enter the war, the president's "lost" Potsdam journal (found in 1978) shows him writing: "Fini Japs when that comes about." And the next day, in an exuberant letter to his wife, Truman wrote that with the Soviet declaration of war, "we'll end the war a year sooner now, and think of the kids who won't be killed!"

It is also obvious that if assurances for the emperor were put forward together with the Soviet attack, the likelihood of an early Japanese surrender would be even greater. The JIC recognized this in its April 29, 1945, report, observing that there first had to be a realization of the "inevitability of defeat," which the JIC judged a Soviet declaration of war would produce. Once "the Japanese people, as well as their leaders, were persuaded both that absolute defeat was inevitable and that unconditional surrender did not imply national annihilation, surrender might follow fairly quickly."

QUESTIONS TO CONSIDER

1. Why does Alperovitz think that it was unnecessary to use the atomic bomb on Japan?

2. Does Alperovitz's description of a gap about what is known by the general public and specialists like himself seem fair or misguided to you? Why?

3. Is Alperovitz's argument persuasive to you? Why or why not?

Why America Dropped the Bomb

BY DONALD KAGAN

Donald Kagan is a professor of history and classics at Yale University. He opposes the revisionist historians who feel that the dropping of the atomic bomb was a political rather than a military act. This article was part of a review of Gar Alperovitz's book The Decision to Use the Atomic Bomb *(1995).*

The 50th anniversary of the use of atomic bombs on Hiroshima and Nagasaki has produced a wholly predictable debate over the necessity and morality of that decision. Or perhaps debate is the wrong word. All too typical of this year's commemorative activities was a proposed exhibit on Hiroshima at the Smithsonian Institution in Washington; the script for this exhibit presented a picture, in the words of an irate *Wall Street Journal* editorial, of a "besieged Japan yearning for peace" and lying "at the feet of an implacably violent enemy—the United States." Although the exhibit was subsequently canceled, it **encapsulated**[1] a point of view that has now endured for a full half-century, and shows no sign of waning.

On August 6, 1945 the American war plane *Enola Gay* dropped an atomic bomb on Hiroshima, killing between 70,000 and 100,000 Japanese. Three days later another atomic device was exploded over Nagasaki. Within a few days Japan surrendered, and the terrible struggle that we call World War II was over.

At the time, the American people cheered the bombings without restraint, and for the simplest of reasons. As the literary historian Paul Fussell, then a combat soldier expecting to take part in the anticipated invasion of Japan, would later recall:

> We learned to our astonishment that we would not be obliged in a few months to rush up the beaches near Tokyo assault-firing while being machine-gunned, mortared, and shelled, and for all the practiced phlegm of our tough facades we broke down and cried with relief and joy. We were going to live.

At that moment, few if any Americans doubted that the purpose of this first use of atomic bombs was to bring the war to the swiftest possible end, and thereby to **avert**[2] American casualties.

But the moment was short-lived. As early as 1946, challenges to the dominant opinion appeared and soon multiplied. . . .

Let us begin with the first line of revisionist attack, which is to question whether an invasion of Japan would have been so costly in American lives as to justify the use of atomic bombs in order to avoid it.

---

[1] **encapsulated**—to encase or put in a small case or covering.

[2] **avert**—prevent the occurrence of, avoid.

In his memoirs, President Truman wrote that an invasion of the Japanese home islands would have entailed the loss of 500,000 American lives. In their own respective memoirs, Secretary of War Henry Stimson and Secretary of State James Byrnes proposed the figure of one million lives, or one million casualties overall. The revisionists have pounced on both these estimates, producing lengthy arguments to show that they are impossible and leaving the impression that the numbers were cut from whole cloth to justify the bombings after the fact. All this is meant to undermine the **probity**[3] of American leaders by showing them to be liars: if anticipated casualties at the time were fewer than the claims made after the war, the revisionists argue, then fear of such casualties could not have been the motive for dropping the bomb.

But some anticipations of casualties at the time were in fact quite high. A study done in August 1944 for the Joint Chiefs of Staff projected that an invasion of Japan would "cost a half-million American lives and many more that number in wounded," while a memorandum from Herbert Hoover to President Truman in May 1945 estimated that a negotiated peace with Japan would "save 500,000 to one million lives." There is every reason to believe that such round, frightening numbers lingered in the minds of Truman and Stimson long after they were first received, and that they haunted all future deliberations.

More precise estimates were made nearer in time to the use of the bombs. In preparation for a meeting with President Truman scheduled for June 18, 1945, the army's Chief of Staff, General George C. Marshall, asked General Douglas MacArthur for a figure of American casualties in the projected invasion of Kyushu (code name: Olympic). Marshall was shocked by MacArthur's

[3] **probity**—uprightness, honesty.

reply: 105,050 battle casualties (dead and wounded) in the first 90 days alone, and another 12,600 casualties among American noncombatants. Marshall called these figures unacceptably high.

In connection with that same meeting on June 18, the document that has received the most attention by revisionists is a study by the Joint War Plans Committee, prepared on June 15. It estimated that casualties in an invasion of southern Kyushu on November 1, followed some months later by an assault on the Tokyo plain, would be a relatively low 40,000 dead, 150,000 wounded, and 3,500 missing, for a total of 193,500 casualties in the entire two-pronged operation.

There are, however, several problems with these estimates. To begin with, they did not include naval casualties, although experience at Okinawa showed these were certain to be numerous. A separate estimate did exist for such losses—9,700 in the Kyushu invasion—but it excluded the unknowable number of casualties that would be suffered by American soldiers and sailors on transports struck by kamikaze attacks. Intercepted Japanese military messages revealed that the Japanese had about 10,000 planes, half of them kamikazes, to defend the home islands. In addition, the Japanese counted on flying bombs, human torpedoes, suicide-attack boats, midget suicide submarines, motorboat bombs, and navy swimmers to be used as human mines. All of these "had been used at Okinawa and the Philippines with lethal results," and the intercepts showed that they were now being placed on Kyushu.

The report offering the figure of 40,000 dead, moreover, was peppered with disclaimers that casualties "are not subject to accurate estimate" and that the estimate was "admittedly only an educated guess." Indeed, when the report went from the original committee up to the Joint planners, it omitted the casualty figures altogether on the grounds that they were "not subject to accurate estimate." The document then went to Assistant Chief of Staff General John E. Hull. In his accompanying memorandum to General Marshall, Hull suggested that losses in the first 30 days in Kyushu would be on the order of those taken at Luzon, or about 1,000 casualties per day. Hull's memorandum, and not the committee report listing specific figures, was read out by Marshall at the June 18 conference with the President.

At the meeting itself, Fleet Admiral William D. Leahy, chairman of the Joint Chiefs, suggested that Luzon was not as sound an analogy as Okinawa. There, American casualties had run to 75,000, or some 35 percent of the attacking force. "Marshall," writes the historian Edward Drea, "allowed that 766,700 assault troops would be employed against Kyushu. Although unstated, a 35-percent casualty rate translated to more than a quarter-million American casualties." As for the President, he was very mindful of the bloodbath at Okinawa, and he demanded the "Joint Chiefs' assurance that an invasion of Kyushu would neither repeat that savagery nor **degenerate**[4] into race war." There is no evidence that Truman ever saw or heard the omitted low figures for the entire operation that had been drawn up by the Joint War Plans Committee.

But whatever the value of any of these estimates, they soon became obsolete. Marshall's calculation rested on the assumption that Kyushu would be defended by eight Japanese divisions, or fewer than 300,000 men, and that American domination of the sea and air would make reinforcement impossible. Intercepts of Japanese military communications soon made a mockery of those expectations. By July 21, the estimate of Japanese troops on Kyushu had grown to 455,000; by the end of the month, to 525,000. Colonel Charles A. Willoughby, MacArthur's intelligence officer, took note of the new

---

[4] **degenerate**—decline in physical, mental, or moral qualities.

situation: "This threatening development, if not checked, may grow to a point where we attack on a ratio of one (1) to one (1), which is not the recipe for victory." Soon the number of Japanese troops on Kyushu rose to 680,000 and, on July 31, a medical estimate projected American battle and nonbattle casualties needing treatment at 394,859. This figure, of course, excluded those killed at once, who would be beyond treatment.

Years later, in a letter, Truman described a meeting in the last week of July at which Marshall suggested the invasion would cost "at a minimum one-quarter-of-a-million casualties, and might cost as much as a million, on the American side alone, with an equal number of the enemy. The other military and naval men present agreed." If Truman's recollection was accurate, this may have been the last such estimate before the dropping of the bomb; but whether accurate or not, there can be no doubt that Marshall's own concern did not abate even after Hiroshima. On the very next day he sent a message to MacArthur expressing alarm at the Japanese strength on southern Kyushu, and asking for alternative invasion sites. On August 11, five days after Hiroshima, three days after the Soviets had entered the war, and two days after Nagasaki, when the Japanese had still not surrendered, Marshall thought it would be necessary "to continue a prolonged struggle" and even raised the possibility of using atomic bombs as tactical weapons against massed enemy troops during the invasion.

As the foregoing suggests, it was, and remains, impossible to make convincing estimates of the casualties to be expected in case of an American invasion of the Japanese home islands. From the beginning the debate has been **tendentious**,[5] distracting attention from more important questions. The large numbers offered by

---

[5] **tendentious**—biased, marked in favor of a particular point of view.

Stimson and Truman in their memoirs may not have been accurate, but the attacks on those numbers by the revisionists are at least as suspect. No one can be sure that the true figure would have been closer to the lower than to the higher estimates.

In any case, what matters is not what American leaders claimed after the war, but what they believed before the atomic bombs were used. On that point, there can be no doubt. In discussions that were not shaped by attempts to justify using the bomb, since it had not yet even been tested, men like Truman, Stimson, and Marshall were deeply worried over the scale of American casualties—whatever their precise number—that were certain to be incurred by an invasion. The President could not face another Okinawa, much less something greater. That is all we need to know to understand why he and his associates were prepared to use the bomb.

Yet this conclusion, supported both by the evidence and by common sense, has been furiously resisted by revisionists and their large cohorts of fellow-travelers. Thus, a 1990 account of the current state of the question reports: "The consensus among scholars is that the bomb was not needed to avoid an invasion of Japan and to end the war within a relatively short time . . . an invasion was a remote possibility." This would have been welcome news indeed to General Marshall, who as we have seen was deeply concerned about the difficulty and human cost of such an invasion right up to the moment of surrender.

A second pillar of the argument that the dropping of the bomb was unnecessary goes as follows. The Japanese had already been defeated, and it was only a brief matter of time before continued conventional bombing and shortages caused by the naval blockade would have made them see reason. They were, in fact, already sending out peace feelers in the hope of ending the war. If the Americans had been more forthcoming, willing to abandon their demand for unconditional surrender and to promise that Japan could retain its emperor, peace could have come without either an invasion *or* the use of the bomb.

This particular case rests in large part on a quite rational evaluation of the condition of Japan and its dismal military prospects in the spring of 1945, and on the evidence that Japanese officials were indeed discussing the possibility of a negotiated peace, using the Soviets as **intermediaries**.[6] But neither of these lines of argument proves the point; nor do both of them taken together.

Even the most diehard military leaders of Japan knew perfectly well how grim their objective situation was. But this did not deter them from continuing the war, as the most reputable study of the Japanese side of the story makes clear. Although they did not expect a smashing and glorious triumph, they were confident of at least winning an operational victory "in the decisive battle for the homeland." Since *any* negotiated peace would be considered a surrender which would split the nation apart, Japan's militarists wanted to put it off as long as possible, and to enter negotiations only on the heels of a victory.

Some thought an American invasion could be repelled. Most hoped to inflict enough damage to make the invaders regroup. Others were even more determined; they "felt that it would be far better to die fighting in battle than to seek an ignominious survival by surrendering the nation and acknowledging defeat."

Premier Kantaro Suzuki supported the army's plan, and was content to prosecute the war with every means at his disposal—for that, after all, was "the way of the warrior and the path of the patriot." At a conference

---

[6] **intermediaries**—go-betweens, persons who act for other persons.

on June 8, 1945, in the presence of the emperor, the Japanese government formally affirmed its policy: "The nation would fight to the bitter end."

In spite of that, some Japanese officials did try to end the war by diplomatic negotiation before it was too late. Early efforts had been undertaken by minor military officials, who approached American OSS officers in Switzerland in April; but they were given no support from Tokyo. In July, some members of the Japanese government thought they could enlist the help of the Soviet Union in negotiating a peace that would not require a surrender or the occupation of the home islands. It is hard to understand why they thought the USSR would want to help a state it disliked and whose territory it coveted, especially when Japanese prospects were at their **nadir**;[7] but such indeed was their hope.

The officials sent their proposals to Naotake Sato, the Japanese ambassador in Moscow. Their messages, and Sato's responses, were intercepted and must have influenced American plans considerably.

Sato warned his **interlocutors**[8] in Tokyo that there was no chance of Soviet cooperation. An entry in the diary of Secretary of the Navy James V. Forrestal for July 15, 1945 reports "the gist of [Sato's] final message . . . Japan was thoroughly and completely defeated and . . . the only course open was quick and definite action recognizing such fact." Sato repeated this advice more than once, but the response from Tokyo was that the war must continue.

Revisionists and others have argued that the United States could have paved the way by dropping the demand for unconditional surrender, and especially that the U.S. should have indicated the emperor would be retained. But intercepts clearly revealed (according to

---

[7] **nadir**—the lowest point.

[8] **interlocutors**—people who take part in a conversation or dialogue.

Gerhard Weinberg in *A World at Arms*) that "the Japanese government would not accept the concept of unconditional surrender even if the institution of the imperial house were preserved." And then there were the intercepts of military messages, which led to the same conclusion—namely, as Edward J. Drea writes, that "the Japanese civil authorities might be considering peace, but Japan's military leaders, who American decision-makers believed had total control of the nation, were preparing for war to the knife."

The demand for unconditional surrender had in any case been asserted by Roosevelt and had become a national rallying cry. Truman could not lightly abandon it, nor is there reason to think that he wanted to. Both he and Roosevelt had clear memories of World War I and how its unsatisfactory conclusion had helped bring on World War II. In the former conflict, the Germans had not surrendered unconditionally; their land had not been occupied; they had not been made to accept the fact of their defeat in battle. Demagogues like Hitler had made use of this opportunity to claim that Germany had not lost but had been "stabbed in the back" by internal traitors like the socialists and the Jews, a technique that made it easier to rouse the Germans for a second great effort. In 1944, Roosevelt said that "practically all Germans deny the fact that they surrendered during the last war, but this time they are going to know it. And so are the Japs."

In the event, Truman did allow the Japanese to keep their emperor. Why did he not announce that intention in advance, to make surrender easier? Some members of the administration thought he should do so, but most feared that any advance **concession**[9] would be taken as a sign of weakness, and encourage the Japanese bitter-enders in their hope that they could win a more favorable peace by holding out. And there were also

---

[9] **concession**—something yielded or given up.

those who were opposed to any policy that would leave the emperor in place. These, as it happens, were among the more liberal members of the administration, men like Dean Acheson and Archibald MacLeish. Their opposition was grounded in the belief that, as MacLeish put it, "the throne [was] an anachronistic, feudal institution, perfectly suited to the manipulation and use of anachronistic, feudal-minded groups within the country." It is also worth pointing out, as did the State Department's Soviet expert, Charles Bohlen, that a concession with regard to the emperor, as well as negotiations in response to the so-called peace feelers on any basis other than unconditional surrender, might well have been seen by the Soviets as a violation of commitments made at Yalta and as an effort to end the war before the Soviet Union could enter it.

What if the U.S. had issued a public warning that it had the atomic bomb, and described its fearful qualities? Or warned the Japanese of the imminent entry of the Soviet Union into the fighting? Or, best of all, combined both warnings with a promise that Japan could keep its emperor? Again, there are no grounds for believing that any or all of these steps would have made a difference to the determined military **clique**[10] that was making Japan's decisions.

Even after the atomic bomb had exploded at Hiroshima on August 6, the Japanese refused to yield. An American announcement clarified the nature of the weapon that had done the damage, and warned that Japan could expect more of the same if it did not surrender. Still, the military held to its policy of resistance and insisted on a delay until a response was received to the latest Japanese approach to the Soviet Union. The answer came on August 8, when the Soviets declared

---

[10] **clique**—a small exclusive group or snobbish set.

war and sent a large army against Japanese forces in Manchuria.

The foolishness of looking to the Soviets was now inescapably clear, but still Japan's leaders took no steps to end the fighting. The Minister of War, General Korechika Anami, went so far as to deny that Hiroshima had been struck by an atomic bomb. Others insisted that the U.S. had used its only bomb there, or that world opinion would prevent the Americans from using any others they might have. Then on August 9 the second atomic bomb fell on Nagasaki, again doing terrible damage.

The Nagasaki bomb convinced even Anami that "the Americans appear to have 100 atomic bombs . . . they could drop three per day. The next target might well be Tokyo." Even so, a meeting of the Imperial Council that night failed to achieve a consensus to accept defeat. Anami himself insisted that Japan continue to fight. If the Japanese people "went into the decisive battle in the homeland determined to display the full measure of patriotism . . . Japan would be able to avert the crisis facing her." The chief of the army general staff, Yoshijiro Umezu, expressed his confidence in the military's "ability to deal a smashing blow to the enemy," and added that in view of the sacrifices made by the many men who had gladly died for the emperor, "it would be inexcusable to surrender unconditionally." Admiral Soemu Toyoda, chief of the navy's general staff, argued that Japan could now use its full air power, heretofore held in reserve in the homeland. Like Anami, he did not guarantee victory, but asserted that "we do not believe that we will be possibly defeated."

These were the views of Japan's top military leaders *after* the explosion of two atomic bombs and the Soviet attack on Manchuria.

Premier Suzuki and the others who were by now favoring peace knew all this was madness. The

Allies would never accept the military's conditions—restrictions on the extent of Japanese disarmament, on the occupation of Japan, and on trials of Japanese leaders for war crimes—and the continuation of warfare would be a disaster for the Japanese people. To break the deadlock he took the extraordinary step of asking the emperor to make the decision. (Normally no proposal was put to the emperor until it had achieved the unanimous approval of the Imperial Council.) At 2 A.M. on August 10, Emperor Hirohito responded to the premier's request by giving his sanction to the acceptance of the Allied terms. The Japanese reply included the proviso that the emperor be retained.

There was still disagreement within the American government on this subject. Public opinion was very hostile to the retention of the emperor, and in particular, as Gerhard Weinberg has written, "the articulate organizations of the American Left" resisted any concessions and "urged the dropping of additional atomic bombs instead." At last, the U.S. devised compromise language that accepted the imperial system by implication, while providing that the Japanese people could establish their own form of government.

Although the Japanese leaders found this acceptable, that was not the end of the matter. Opponents of peace tried to reverse the decision by a *coup d'état*. They might have succeeded had General Anami supported them, but he was unwilling to defy the emperor's orders. He solved his dilemma by committing suicide, and the plot failed. Had it succeeded, the war would have continued to a bloody end, with Japan under the brutal rule of a fanatical military clique. Some idea of the thinking of this faction is provided by an intercept of an August 15 message to Tokyo from the commander of Japan's army in China:

> Such a disgrace as the surrender of several million troops without fighting is not paralleled

in the world's military history, and it is absolutely
impossible to submit to the unconditional surrender of a million picked troops in perfectly
healthy shape . . . .

It was the emperor, then, who was decisive in causing
Japan to surrender. What caused him to act in so
remarkable a way? He was moved by the bomb—and
by the Soviet declaration of war. (That declaration,
scheduled for August 15, was itself hastened by the use
of the bomb, and moved up to August 8.) But statements
by the emperor and premier show clearly that they
viewed the Soviet invasion as only another wartime set-
back. It was the bomb that changed the situation entirely.

On hearing of this terrible new weapon, Emperor
Hirohito said, "We must put an end to the war as speedily as possible so that this tragedy will not be repeated."
Suzuki said, plainly, that Japan's "war aim had been lost
by the enemy's use of the new-type bomb." Finally, the
central role of the bomb was made graphically clear in
the Imperial Rescript of August 14, in which the emperor
explained to his people the reasons for the surrender. At
its heart was the following statement:

The enemy has begun to employ a new and
most cruel bomb, the power of which to do
damage is indeed incalculable, taking the toll of
many innocent lives. Should we continue to
fight, it would not only result in an ultimate collapse and obliteration of the Japanese nation,
but it would also lead to the total extinction of
human civilization. Such being the case, how are
We to save the millions of Our subjects . . . ? This
is the reason why We have ordered the acceptance of the provisions of the Joint Declaration
of the Powers.

There can be, in short, no doubt that the actual use of atomic weapons was critical in bringing a swift end to the war, and that mere warnings would not have sufficed.

QUESTIONS TO CONSIDER

1. Why was it so important for the United States to avoid having to invade the Japanese home islands?

2. What part did the Japanese emperor play in ending the war? Was it decisive? Explain your answer.

3. How balanced do you think Kagan is in his presentation of the arguments about the use of the atomic bomb? Point to specific details that support your answer.

The Scientists:
Their Views
20 Years Later

BY WILLIAM L. LAURENCE

Twenty years after the atomic bombings, William L. Laurence, the New York Times correspondent who had reported on the bomb project and flown on the Nagasaki mission, interviewed many of the key scientists and leaders involved with the atomic bomb. He asked them, "Knowing what you do now, would you do the same again?" The answer was invariably yes.

"WHY DID YOU HELP MAKE THE BOMB?"

"Knowing what you do now, would you do the same again?"

Repeatedly, the scientists and the military and civilian leaders who participated in the decision to build and use the atomic bomb are asked such questions. A number of the leading protagonists have died during the past two decades. The dead, all of whom agreed that the bomb be used without prior warning or demonstration, include Enrico Fermi, Ernest O. Laurence and Arthur H. Compton, among the scientists; Sir Winston Churchill, Henry L. Stimson, General George C. Marshall, Admiral Ernest King and General Henry H. Arnold, among the civilian and military leaders. Very few who played equal roles in arriving at the great decision are left. Hence the twentieth anniversary of the fateful date on which the decision was carried out over Hiroshima suggested itself as a **propitious**[1] time for asking leading representatives among these survivors whether, in contemplating the past in the light of more recent knowledge, they would do it again. The men and their replies:

DR. J. ROBERT OPPENHEIMER

[Director, Institute for Advanced Study, Princeton, N.J. Headed the Los Alamos team—the greatest scientific team ever assembled—which designed, developed and fabricated the atomic bomb. Later opposed the development of the hydrogen bomb.]

Q.: After what has happened during these past twenty years, would you, under conditions as they were in 1942, accept once again the invitation to work on the development of the atomic bomb?
A.: Yes.

Q.: Even after Hiroshima?
A.: Yes.

Q.: Do you think it was necessary to drop the two atomic bombs over Japan when Japan was already on her knees?
A.: From what I know today, I do not believe that we could have known with any degree of certainty that the

---

[1] **propitious**—favorable.

atomic bomb was necessary to end the war. But that was not the view of those who had studied the situation at the time and who were thinking of an invasion of Japan. Probably they were wrong. Japan had already approached Moscow to sound out the United States about terms of peace. Probably a settlement could have been reached by political means. But the men who made the decision— and I am thinking particularly of Secretary [of War Henry L.] Stimson and President Truman—were sure that the choice was either invasion or the bomb. Maybe they were wrong, but I am not sure that Japan was ready to surrender.

Dr. Oppenheimer added:

I never regretted, and do not regret now, having done my part of the job. I have a deep, continuing, haunting sense of the damage done to European culture by the two world wars. The existence of the bomb has reduced the chance of World War III and has given us valid hope.

I believe it was an error that Truman did not ask Stalin to carry on further talks with Japan, and also that the warning to Japan was completely inadequate.

But I also think that it was a damn good thing that the bomb was developed, that it was recognized as something important and new, and that it would have an effect on the course of history. In that world, in that war, it was the only thing to do. I only regret that it was not done two years earlier. It would have saved a million or more lives.

DR. EDWARD TELLER

[Lawrence Radiation Laboratories of the University of California at Berkeley. A member of the Los Alamos team. Known as "the father of the hydrogen bomb."]

To develop the bomb was right. To drop it was wrong. We could have used the bomb to end the war without bloodshed by exploding it high over Tokyo at night without prior warning. If it had been exploded at an altitude of 20,000 feet, instead of the low altitude of 2,000 feet (as was the case at Hiroshima and Nagasaki), there would have been a minimum loss of life, if any, and hardly any damage to property, but there would have been tremendous sound and light effects. We could then have said to the Japanese leaders: "This was an atomic bomb. One of them can destroy a city. Surrender or be destroyed!"

I believe they would have surrendered just as they did following the destruction of the two cities. If that had happened it would have been a tremendous moral as well as military victory. We could have said to the world: "See what science can do? It has ended the war without shedding a drop of blood!" On the other hand, if they had failed to surrender they would have given us good reason for using the bomb as we did, though we might have waited a longer interval before we dropped the second bomb.

Like most of the other scientists, Dr. Teller worked on the bomb because he believed we were in a race against the Nazi scientists. But, he said:

Even when it was found out that there was no race, I still wanted to continue working on the bomb as an instrument to end the war, but without unnecessary bloodshed.

Dr. Teller added:

I was positive then, and I am positive now, that we made a mistake dropping the bomb without a previous bloodless demonstration. But I am quite willing to work on such a project again because I believe that in a democratic government such mistakes are the exception rather than the rule.

To **abstain**[2] from progress is a **medieval**[3] idea. I am in favor of any advance in knowledge or any development of the greater power of man. I believe in such advances because I feel that on the whole they will be used in the right way by democratic nations.

Does a scientist have a choice? In an emergency, it is obvious that everyone's choice is more restricted. The pressures are greatly increased. Everyone's responsibility is greater. However, an emergency does not eliminate any individual's responsibility, choice or conscience.

DR. EUGENE P. WIGNER

[Princeton University. One of the group, led by Enrico Fermi, who lighted the first atomic pile under a squash court at the University of Chicago on December 2, 1942. The only winner of the world's three major honors in physics—the Fermi Award of the U.S. Atomic Energy Commission, the Atoms for Peace Award and the Nobel Prize.]

On the basis of admittedly scant information at the time the use of the nuclear weapon against Japan was contemplated, I came to the conclusion that Japan would surrender without its use, and that such use was unnecessary. For this reason I signed the so-called Franck petition [the report of a group of scientists headed by James Franck, Nobel Prize winner in physics, opposing the use of the bomb].

Subsequently, particularly as a result of my reading Herbert Feis's book *Japan Subdued,* serious doubts concerning this question have been raised in my mind. I am now inclined to believe that the use of the nuclear bomb to terminate the war was a more humane way and led to less suffering and loss of life than any other way that was contemplated.

---

[2] **abstain**—to do without something voluntarily.

[3] **medieval**—having to do with the Middle Ages; primitive or barbaric.

There was no difference in my attitude concerning the possible use of a nuclear weapon against Germany, on the one hand, and against Japan, on the other. In both cases my attitude would have been governed at that time by the view of whether peace could be obtained without the use of a nuclear weapon.

I signed the Franck petition because I believed at the time that it would be possible to terminate the war without the use of the nuclear weapon. Today I would try to avoid responsibility for using it or not using it. I would leave it to other people to decide, on the grounds that it was not my job.

As for my participation in making the bomb, there was no choice. The original discovery that made it possible was made in Germany, and we had believed that the German scientists were ahead of us in the development of a nuclear weapon. I shudder to think what would have happened if Germany had been first to acquire the weapon.

I had volunteered for the Army as a soldier, but was refused. I knew I had to leave the ivory tower and go out into the world, because what was at stake in the war was just too much.

Believing as I did that the use of the weapon was unnecessary, I was very unhappy about it, and I would have been equally unhappy had I believed that it was necessary to use it. But I had no sense of guilt, since I did not make the decision.

The scientist in a democracy has the right to refuse to do anything distasteful to him. But as long as scientists in totalitarian countries have no such choice, it would not be right to exercise such legal rights for, if one did, there soon would not be any democracy. The scientist, like any other civilian, should not act in such a way as to make democracy impossible.

DR. EMILIO SEGRE

[University of California at Berkeley. One of Fermi's original associates at the University of Rome. Winner of the Nobel Prize in Physics.]

Q.: If you knew then what you know now, would you have worked on the bomb?

A.: Under the circumstances prevailing at the time, yes. We had Hitler around. We knew the Nazis would make the bomb and were working on it. We would have been crazy not to make the bomb under the circumstances. We could not be sure atomic bombs would not start dropping on us. If that had happened, Hitler would have won the war.

Q.: Did you approve the use of the bomb?

A.: The President had hardly any alternative. On the basis of the information available—the probability that the war would go on for a long time—I thought, and still think, the decision was the only one possible. But I am glad I was not the President.

DR. LUIS W. ALVAREZ

[University of California at Berkeley. Played a major role on the Los Alamos team and served as a key member of the group that assembled the two nuclear weapons on Tinian. Flew aboard the B-29 *Enola Gay* on its atomic-bomb run over Hiroshima.]

Q.: Did you approve the use of the bomb in 1945?

A.: Of course. We had been in the war a long time. It seemed certain to continue for a long time, with enormous loss of life on both sides. We had the means to end the war quickly, with a great saving of human life. I believed it was the only sensible thing to do, and I still do.

Q.: Would you do it over again? Would you still work on the bomb?

A.: Of course. The weapon was possible. So far as we knew, we were in a race with the Germans. We had to beat them to it, or risk losing the war.

Q.: Would you have done it, knowing subsequent history?

A.: Yes. I am proud to have had a part in a program that by most modem estimates saved a million lives, both Japanese and American, that would otherwise have been lost in the projected invasion. This pride is reinforced by the knowledge that the world has not had a major war in the past 20 years, and that most responsible people feel the risk of a World War III has diminished steadily with time in these same years. I am confident that both of these admirable situations are directly traceable to the existence of nuclear weapons.

LIEUTENANT GENERAL
LESLIE R. GROVES U.S.A. RET.

[As head of the Manhattan Project, in less than two and a half years built the $2 billion industrial empire which produced the atomic bomb on schedule.]

There was never any question as to the use of the bomb, if it was successfully developed, on the part of anyone who was in a top position on the project and who knew what was going on. One group that objected to the use of the bomb did not object until after V-E Day. That group was mostly centered around people who were bitterly anti-Germany and who did not appear to feel the same way toward Japan.

JOHN J. MCCLOY

[Attorney and civic leader. Former U.S. Military Governor and High Commissioner for Germany. As Assistant Secretary of War under Stimson, participated in the wartime inner councils.]

Q.: We made the A-bomb because we believed we were in a race with the Nazis. Would we have made it if we had known, as we know now, that the Nazis were actually very far from making the A-bomb?

A: Yes, we would have done it because of the mere fact that atomic energy was in the air. I don't believe you could have checked it. We couldn't afford to take a chance that somebody wouldn't come along and do it.

We were in a race with ideas. At that stage, under the pressure of war, we would have gone ahead anyway. Here there was something to end the war, to bring about peace, to prevent war in the future.

Q.: Knowing what you know today, would you approve dropping the bomb as we did?

A.: I tried to tell Stimson to advise the Japanese that we had the bomb. I am absolutely convinced that had we said they could keep the Emperor, together with the threat of the atomic bomb, they would have accepted and we would never have had to drop the bomb.

However, if they had refused our offer, then there is no question that we should have used the bomb.

The final decision was that there was no alternative; that neither air bombardment nor blockade would end the war. It was either invasion or the bomb. It was decided not to mention the bomb because it was still not known whether it would work (it was before Alamogordo[4]) and because there was at that time an inhibition against talking about it.

Under the circumstances we had to go ahead with it, because an invasion would have cost terrible casualties. However, I wish we had given them better notice about the Emperor and the bomb. Then our position before the world would have been better.

---

[4] Alamogordo—site in New Mexico of one of the atomic bomb tests.

As to my own position, it was to bring the war to an end sooner than it would otherwise be ended, and thus to save American lives. We were losing about 250 men a day in the Pacific. The estimated American casualties for landing on Japanese shores were anywhere between 250,000 and 1,000,000, while the Japanese casualties were conservatively estimated to run as high as 10 million. We were therefore faced with a very serious question: Should we go on with the war and face the American soldiers who were subjected to unnecessary danger and the families of all those who were killed after we could have stopped the war?

The reason that we did not have a demonstration of the bomb was, first, that it would have completely wiped out the element of surprise, which in my opinion was extremely important. As it turned out, that was one of the reasons why Japan surrendered so quickly. They weren't prepared for it. It was a bolt out of heaven. There has never been a surprise to equal it since the Trojan horse.[5]

Also, if we had had a demonstration or warning, and if neither had any effect—and I don't believe they would have—then the Japanese would have made every effort to see that the plane that carried the bomb was brought down, and it would have increased the hazards of the men who were carrying the bomb manyfold.

Above all else was the very strong feeling on the part of President Truman, which was the same feeling that the rest of us who knew about it had, that it was criminal and morally wrong for us to have means to bring this war to a proper conclusion and then not use the means.

It is true we didn't need the bomb to win, but we needed it to save American lives.

---

[5] Trojan horse—huge wooden horse inside which Greek soldiers hid and were brought into the city of Troy during the Trojan War for a sneak attack.

Remember this, that when the bomb was used, before it was used and at the time it was used, we had no basic concept of the damage that it would do. We thought it would do a great deal, but we didn't know at that time whether the explosion might not be a little too high or a little too low. We didn't know whether the fusing would work. The bomb used over Hiroshima had never been tested. A lot of features had been tested, but only of the gun-part—it was a gun-type bomb in which a projectile of uranium 285 was fired into a uranium 235 target. We had no real knowledge that the thing would work. The fact that the bomb had exploded at Alamogordo—the **implosion**[6] type, the kind used over Nagasaki—was no indication that the Hiroshima type would go off.

Also, the one tested in New Mexico was put up on a tower. It had none of the mechanisms that were necessary to set it off at the proper height. The actual **proximity**[7] fusing for control of the height at which it would be exploded was tested in the United States about 48 hours before it was actually used over Nagasaki. It was tested over the Tinian area 24 hours ahead of time. And nobody could tell just what was going to happen, and particularly we couldn't tell how severe the explosion would be and how many people would be injured.

The decisions recommending the use of the bomb, made by the interim committee formed by President Truman, were reached after thorough exploration of every possible angle: Could you have a demonstration? What would that mean? How and where would you have a demonstration? What would be its effects? We had not at that time seen the explosion at Alamogordo, but I can just say that if I had been a Japanese observer and had seen the bomb go off at Alamogordo, I would not have

---

[6] **implosion**—bursting or exploding inward.

[7] **proximity**—nearness, closeness.

advised surrender. It's one thing to see something go off, causing no damage at all but creating a great ball of fire and obviously of tremendous power, but it's another thing to say: "Well, now, they set this off on a tower; maybe it weighs 50 tons. How do we know they can deliver it? That they can get all the mechanisms perfected to deliver it?" And I am sure that anyone who was a sound thinker would have said: "No, that doesn't convince us. In the first place, would they have another?" For example, the German scientists believed that it would be impossible for us to make an atomic bomb, and that if we did we could make only one. The Germans thought of an atomic bomb as something that would have to contain as much as 20 tons of uranium 235, a practically impossible quantity.

QUESTIONS TO CONSIDER

1. Why do the participants generally not regret their part in the creation and use of the atomic bomb?

2. Do you see a difference in guilt between those who developed the bomb and those who ordered its use? Why or why not?

3. Do you agree with Robert Oppenheimer's statement that the "existence of the bomb has reduced the chance of World War III and has given us valid hope"? Why or why not?

Smithsonian Scuttles Enola Gay Exhibit

BY EUGENE L. MEYER AND JACQUELINE TRESCOTT

Fifty years after the dropping of the first atomic bomb on Hiroshima, the Smithsonian Institution, in Washington, D.C., decided to honor the event by mounting an exhibition that examined the bombing in light of four decades of historical research. The exhibition, entitled "The Last Act: The Atomic Bomb and the End of World War II," caused a huge controversy among historians, veterans, and politicians. In the end the exhibit was canceled by the Smithsonian, proving how divisive questions about the use of the atomic bombs remain in the United States.

Smithsonian Secretary I. Michael Heyman yesterday scrapped a controversial exhibit about the atomic bombing of Japan, replacing it with a drastically scaled-down display consisting of the plane that dropped the bomb on Hiroshima, a video about its crew and **minimal**[1] text.

Heyman asserted that the planned exhibit was fundamentally flawed and "consuming me and the institution." He said the forward **fuselage**[2] of the B-29 Enola Gay will be exhibited starting in May at the Smithsonian's National Air and Space Museum without text that would have raised questions about the morality of the decision to drop the bomb.

Despite Heyman's action, the 3.1 million-member American Legion said congressional hearings on the publicly supported Smithsonian Institution should go forward as planned.

Explaining his decision, Heyman said there was a "fundamental flaw in the concept" of the exhibit, titled "The Final Act: The Atomic Bomb and the End of World War II." "Despite our sincere efforts to address everyone's concerns, we were bound to fail," he said. "I have concluded that we made a basic error in attempting to couple a historical treatment of the use of atomic weapons with the 50th anniversary commemoration of the end of the war."

However, Heyman said he is considering "a series of **symposia**"[3] to be held later on the issues raised by atomic weapons and their use. Such panels would involve experts, **curators**,[4] military historians, representatives of veterans and peace groups and others.

---

[1] **minimal**—the least possible.

[2] **fuselage**—the body of an airplane.

[3] **symposia**—a collection of opinions or articles gathered on a specific subject for a specific occasion.

[4] **curators**—persons in charge of museums or museum exhibits.

Heyman also announced a joint forum with the University of Michigan this spring on how museums should handle controversial subjects. He said the forum in Ann Arbor will focus on the Smithsonian's "role and responsibilities as a national museum."

The secretary, who assumed office in September, said he has a "number of regrets about this sad situation." For the past year, veterans, historians and others have argued over the exhibit's contents. Critics charged that the proposed text portrayed the Japanese as innocent victims of **ruthless**[5] Americans determined to avenge Pearl Harbor. The text raised questions about whether the bombing was necessary to avoid a costly invasion of Japan.

World War II ended with Japan's surrender within days of the bombings of Hiroshima and Nagasaki. Heyman said he regretted the controversy had "gotten in the way of the commemoration of our nation's victory over aggression 50 years ago." He also regretted that it has "led some to doubt the value of historical inquiry by museums."

Heyman spoke at a packed news conference attended by more than 100 reporters in the Smithsonian's underground S. Dillon Ripley Center. Not since the 1992 announcement of a "Star Trek" exhibit had a Smithsonian press event been so heavily covered, officials said.

The secretary was flanked by 14 of the institution's 16 governing regents. "As you can see, they stand behind me," he said. The press briefing followed a regularly scheduled regents meeting that lasted three hours.

Conspicuously absent from the briefing was Air and Space Museum Director Martin O. Harwit, whose removal was demanded by 81 members of Congress last week for his role in overseeing the exhibit planning.

---

[5] **ruthless**—having no sympathy or pity.

Mike Fetters, a museum spokesman, said Harwit would have no comment.

Asked about Harwit's future, Heyman said, "One doesn't make personnel decisions that have basic impacts on people's lives and careers in the middle of passion and heat." But he pledged to "look with great care at the management of Air and Space in an organized way."

He may have some help from both houses of Congress, which are planning separate hearings on the Enola Gay controversy and the operations of the Smithsonian.

Sen. Thad Cochran (R-Miss.), a newly appointed regent and a member of the Senate Rules Committee, said he expects the hearings to go forward, but with perhaps a different slant.

"I may suggest to [committee chairman] Senator Ted Stevens that since the Enola Gay has been resolved . . . that we look at how the Smithsonian will be managed in the future and what standards will be developed for interpretative exhibitions," Cochran said.

William M. Detweiler, national commander of the American Legion, said, "The institution has been badly damaged . . . by its own mismanagement and zeal for revisionist history." The Legion had conducted line-by-line negotiations with Smithsonian officials over the proposed exhibit but ultimately demanded its cancellation.

Heyman's action may be an exercise in damage control, but clearly it didn't satisfy everyone. Said Byron Hollinshead, publisher of the military history magazine *MHQ* and a supporter of the decision to drop the bomb: "I think it's a terrible decision for a major historical organization to opt out" of an exhibit fully dealing with the event.

The 180,000-member Air Force Association, a critic of the exhibit-in-the-making for a year, said it would withhold judgment until the scaled-down version opens. "We're encouraged, but we've been there before," said AFA spokesman Jack Giese. "It's wait and see."

Peace groups were also unhappy with the decision not to show the human impact of the two atomic bombs that killed an estimated 140,000 people.

With the exhibit **truncated**,[6] said Robert K. Musil, policy director for the Physicians for Social Responsibility, visitors will fail to learn about high-level **dissenters**[7] of President Harry S. Truman's decision to drop the bomb.

Also missing, Musil said, will be the concerns of scientists at the time that use of the bomb would trigger a nuclear arms race, as well as the story of American veterans "forced to march under atomic test clouds" who later were stricken with cancers he attributed to radiation.

But Heyman said: "I think the new exhibition should be a much simpler one, essentially a display, permitting the Enola Gay and its crew to speak for themselves . . . with labels that don't get into the wisdom, necessity and morality of using atomic weapons."

The Enola Gay has been part of the Smithsonian's collection since 1948. It sat unprotected at Andrews Air Force Base for years before being moved to a Suitland storage facility. There, over the past 12 years, the plane has undergone a $1 million restoration.

Plans call for displaying the entire aircraft at a future extension of the Air and Space Museum at Dulles International Airport. The front portion now sits inside the museum on the Mall.

In repeatedly revising the ill-fated exhibit, Heyman said Air and Space had spent $296,000—about half the

---

[6] **truncated**—having the edges cut off or shortened.

[7] **dissenters**—those who disagree or differ in opinion.

total budgeted for the event. "Not all is lost," he said of the preparations. "Some might be usable. "

But the exhibit catalogue of text and photos, already promoted on the spring list of the Smithsonian Institution Press, won't appear, he said. Other than the "100-plus copies of various scripts circulating," he said, "there is nothing we will print in that regard."

QUESTIONS TO CONSIDER

1. Why did veterans of World War II object so strongly to the proposed exhibit?

2. Why were peace groups dissatisfied with the proposed exhibit?

3. Why do you think there is so much controversy about an event that took place more than half a century ago?

Nagasaki

Three days after the bombing of Hiroshima, a second atomic bomb destroyed the city of Nagasaki, killing more than 25,000 people.

Before

Before and After These two photographs show images of Nagasaki immediately before and just after the blast.

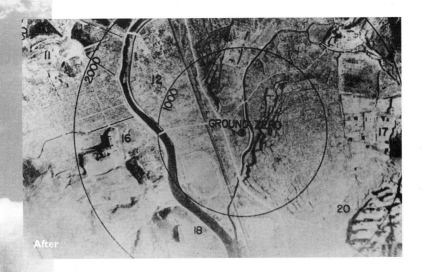

After

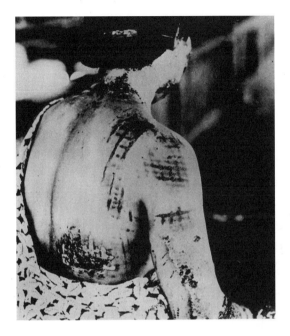

▲

Patterns So intense was the heat that images of patterns were left on buildings (see "The Shadow") and people's skin. Here a woman's skin is burned in a pattern of the kimino she was wearing at the time of the explosion.

◄ **Burn Victims** Each atomic bomb blast unleashed an enormous heat blast that burned the skin on contact.

Rubble Buildings were reduced to rubble in a matter of seconds from the force of the blast. Here a dead horse lies under the cart it was pulling when the bomb hit.

Ruined City As in Hiroshima, the atomic bomb blast flattened buildings, leaving the city in ruins.
▼

Less Damage Even though the plutonium-type bomb carried more force, the mountains around Nagasaki and smaller size of the city resulted in less devastation than in Hiroshima. About the only thing left standing were buildings made of reinforced concrete.

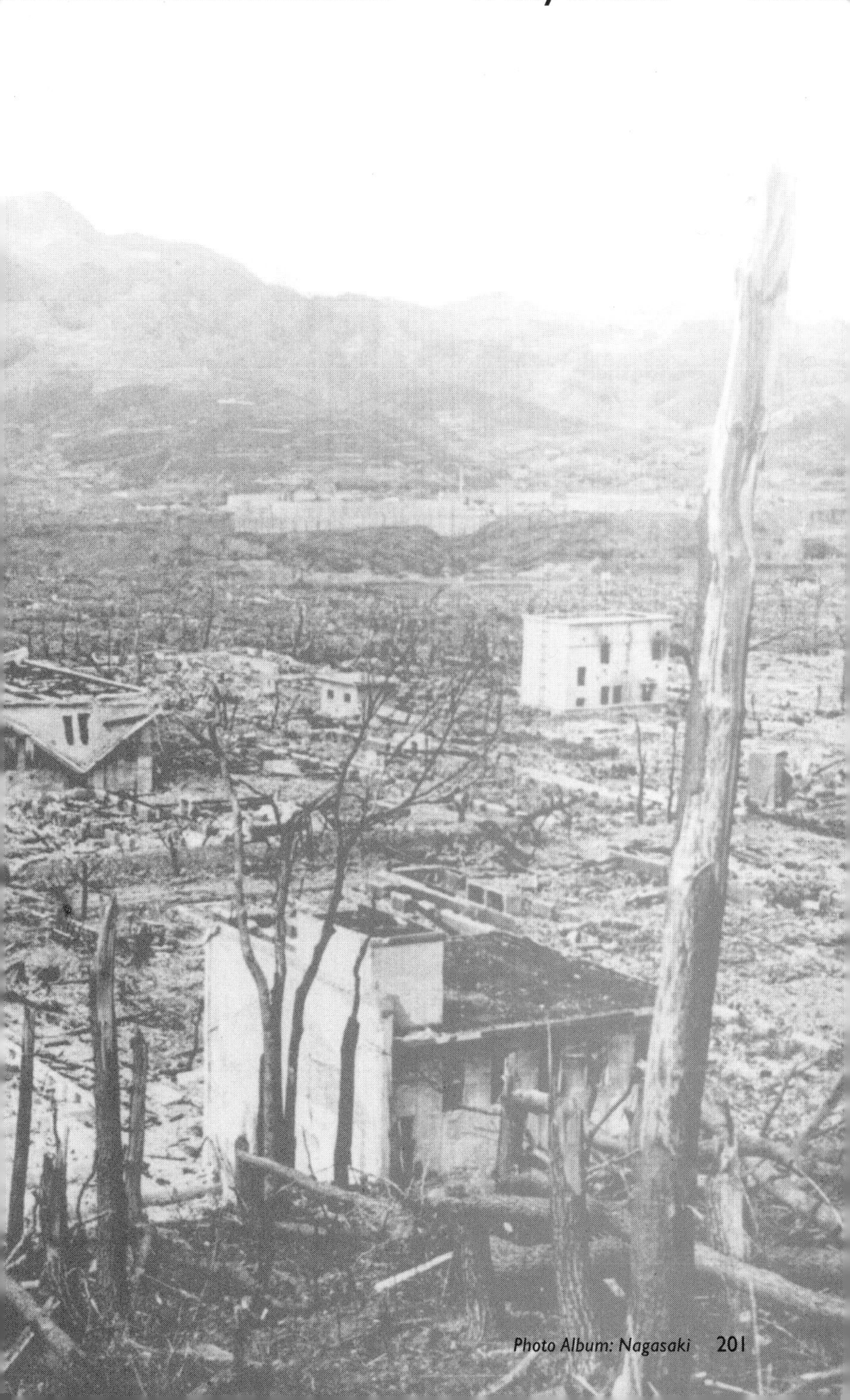

Response to
the Bomb

When the Vacation Is Over for Good

BY MARK STRAND

Mark Strand (1934–) is one of the most important and innova-
tive poets in America. His finest books, Reasons for Moving
(1968) and The Late Hour *(1978), contain meditations of re-*
freshing clarity. He was poet laureate of the United States in
1991. Note the series of puns Strand has included in this poem
about use of nuclear weapons.

It will be strange.
Knowing at last it couldn't go on forever,
The certain voice telling us over and over
That nothing would change.

And remembering too,
Because by then it will all be done with, the way
Things were, and how we had wasted time as though
There was nothing to do,

When, in a flash
The weather turned, and the lofty air became
Unbearably heavy, the wind strikingly dumb
And our cities like ash,

And knowing also,
What we never suspected, that it was something like
   summer
At its most **august**[1] except that the nights were
   warmer
And the clouds seemed to glow,

And even then,
Because we will not have changed much, wondering
   what
Will become of things, and who will be left to do it
All over again,

And somehow trying,
But still unable, to know just what it was
That went so completely wrong, or why it is
We are dying.

---

[1] **august**—inspiring reverence or admiration; majestic.

QUESTIONS TO CONSIDER

1. What is happening at the moment when Strand's poem is occurring?

2. What is the mood of the poem?

3. Does Strand's poem reflect the experiences of people who survived the atomic bombing of Hiroshima? Why or why not?

4. How would you describe Strand's view of the use of atomic weapons? What details from the poem helped you infer this?

On Human Dignity

BY KENZABURO OE

Kenzaburo Oe (1935–) has been one of most important writers in the postwar period in Japan. His writings have particularly explored Japan's struggle to come to terms with the events of World War II. Oe is best known for his novels A Personal Matter *(1964) and* The Silent Cry *(1974) and was awarded the Nobel Prize for literature in 1994. In this selection, Oe describes his annual visit to Hiroshima to attend ceremonies commemorating the dropping of the atomic bomb.*

In the broadest context of human life and death, those of us who happened to escape the atomic holocaust must see Hiroshima as part of all Japan, and as part of all the world. If we survivors want to atone for the "Hiroshima" within us and to give it some positive value, then we should mobilize all efforts against nuclear arms under the maxims "the human misery of Hiroshima" and "the restoration of all humanity." Some people may hold to the fairy-tale view, in this highly politicized age, that the new **acquisition**[1] of nuclear arms by one country actually advances the cause of nuclear disarmament. Since the world has in fact taken the initial step forward in that direction, there may be some ultimate possibility of completely eradicating nuclear weapons.

I cannot, however, overlook the fact that the first actual step toward the non-nuclear dream has virtually crushed the hope for self-recovery of the girls who, ashamed of their **keloids**,[2] are presently wasting their youth in the dark back rooms of Hiroshima. Moreover, there is no clear prospect of the complete **abolition**[3] of nuclear arms. How harsh this situation is for the people of Hiroshima! I hardly have the nerve to probe their feelings.

To put the matter plainly and bluntly, people everywhere on this earth are trying to forget Hiroshima and the unspeakable tragedy perpetrated there. We naturally try to forget our personal tragedies, serious or trifling, as soon as possible (even something as petty as being scorned or disdained by a stranger on a street corner). We try not to carry these things over to tomorrow. It is not strange, therefore, that the whole human race is trying to put Hiroshima, the extreme point of human tragedy, completely out of mind. Without bothering to thumb through public school textbooks, we know that grown-ups make no effort to convey their memories of Hiroshima to their children. All who fortunately survived, or at least luckily suffered no radiation injury, seek to forget the ones who, even now, are struggling painfully *toward* death. Forgetting all these things, we go on living comfortably in the crazy world of the late twentieth century.

---

[1] **acquisition**—act of acquiring or taking possession of.

[2] **keloid**—a red, raised formation of scar tissue caused by excessive tissue repair.

[3] **abolition**—the doing away with, ending.

In October 1964, when a young man born in Hiroshima on the A-bomb day was selected as the last runner to carry the Olympic flame, an American journalist—who has translated some Japanese literature and might be expected to understand Japan and the Japanese people—publicly stated his opinion that this was an unhappy choice because it reminded the Americans of the atomic bomb. If the selected runner had had keloid scars or some other sign of radiation injury, that is, if he had been an unmistakable A-bomb casualty, then I would not object to the selection; an A-bomb victim (if fortunate enough to have lived for these twenty years) would have been more representative of those born on the day of the atomic bombing. But the middle-distance runner actually chosen had a perfectly healthy body; we were impressed by his **stamina**[4] as he ran at full speed in the huge stadium, with the smile of one free of all anxiety. I blessed this young man's perfectly healthy body for the sake of Dr. Shigeto who is already at work on the "problem of the next generation of A-bomb victims."

Still, the American journalist was displeased because the young man, born in Hiroshima on the atomic bombing day, reminded Americans of the atomic bomb. He preferred to erase all traces of Hiroshima from the American memory. Worse still, this preference occurs not only to the American mind. Do not all leaders and peoples who at present possess nuclear weapons also wish to erase Hiroshima from their memories? As the white paper[5] on A-bomb victims and damages seeks to make clear, Hiroshima is the prime example not of the power of atomic weapons but of the misery they cause. But we want to put that aside and get on with living. This attitude is common around the world.

---

[4] **stamina**—power to sustain or go on, ability to resist or recover from fatigue, illness, etc.

[5] white paper—official report.

Powerful leaders in the East and in the West insist on maintaining nuclear arms as a means of preserving the peace. There may be some room for various observations and rationales regarding the possible usefulness of nuclear weapons in preserving true peace; indeed, printing presses all over the world are running off such arguments with all haste. But it is obvious that all advocates of usefulness base their opinions on the *power* of nuclear arms. Such is the fashion and common sense of today's world. Who, then, would want to remember Hiroshima as the **extremity**[6] of human misery?

Not infrequently I encounter A-bomb victims in Hiroshima who say that they want to forget the atomic bomb and do not want to discuss its awesome blast and flash. As for the Olympic flame case, if anyone has the right to protest that the selected runner was an unpleasant reminder of the atomic bomb, the bomb's victims can lay first claim to that right. More than anyone, they would like to forget the horrors of that day. Indeed, they need to forget in order to get on with everyday living. In university I had a friend from Hiroshima; and during our four years together, I never heard him talk about the atomic bomb. Of course, he had a right to remain silent about it.

In Hiroshima at dawn on A-bomb Memorial Day, I have often seen many women standing silently, with deep, dark, fearful eyes, at the Memorial Cenotaph and similar places. On such occasions, I recalled some lines by the Russian poet Yevtushenko.[7]

Her motionless eyes had no expression;
Yet there was something there, sorrow
   or agony,
Inexpressible,
   but something terrible.

---

[6] **extremity**—the very end, farthest possible place.

[7] Yevgeny Yevtushenko (1933–), Russian poet who opposed the oppressive Soviet government. His most famous work is the protest poem "Babi Yar."

Had I spoken to the women, they would have remained silent. They, too, have a right to silence. They have the right, if possible, to forget everything about Hiroshima. They have had enough of Hiroshima. Some A-bomb victims, knowing that the best medical treatment of A-bomb symptoms is available in Hiroshima, nonetheless choose to live elsewhere because they want to get away from all that Hiroshima represents, inwardly and outwardly. Again, they have the right, if possible, to escape Hiroshima completely.

If, however, a victim develops symptoms of an A-bomb related disease, then he can neither forget nor escape Hiroshima. He can, of course, live without thinking about Hiroshima, as far as possible, even if he is a patient in the A-bomb Hospital. If, in addition to removing Hiroshima entirely from his consciousness, the patient could recover fully and move far away from Hiroshima, never to return again, he would be most fortunate. Indeed, if all patients could do so, how wonderful it would be!

Mr. Sadao Miyamoto, however, was a patient who participated in the anti-nuclear movement at risk to his already fragile life. He consciously accepted Hiroshima. He dared to remember history's worst human misery, and he wrote down his reflections on it. He spoke freely, but with some humor, about it to foreigners who frequently visited the hospital. Rather than escape Hiroshima, he accepted it. For whose sake? For the sake of all other human beings, for all who would remain after he met his own miserable death. His passion stemmed from his frank recognition that his own death was inevitable. Mr. Sankichi Tōge[8], that excellent poet, also died in Hiroshima; it was after he had a hemorrhage of the lungs (eventually fatal) that he participated passionately in political activities. "The cruel lung

---

[8] Tōge Sankichi—Japanese poet who survived the bombing of Hiroshima. See "The Shadow" on pages 219–221.

hemorrhage suffered by Mr. Tōge in April 1949 made him struggle against the terror of death . . . [and] decide to join the Japan Communist Party" (testimony of Mr. Kiyoshi Toyota).

If survivors would overcome their fear of death, they too must see some way of giving meaning to their own death. Thus, the dead can survive as part of the lives of those who still live. Gambling on life after death and taking an active role in the hospital was the way taken by Mr. Miyamoto; political participation and joining the Communist Party was Mr. Tōge's way. What terrifies me is that we are completely wasting their death gambles. Mr. Miyamoto seems to have suspected that we would. It bothers me no end to think of this waste. And do not we survivors refuse to gamble on our deaths for fear that we will have to pay off as losers?

Instead of "the dead," I prefer to call these people "saints." They had no religion, and the poet was a Communist. But I think the term "saint" is appropriate for them, in the sense that Albert Camus once put it. "I am intrigued by the question of how I can become a saint." "But you don't believe in God, do you?" "So, can one become a saint without God's help?—that's the only concrete question I know today."

If there are those who dislike the word "saint," then I do not mind remembering these two men, who refused to keep silent unto death, in terms of the following lines by Céline,[9] written in a tougher vein:

The ultimate defeat is, in short, to forget; especially to forget those who kill us. It is to die without any suspicion, to the very end, of how perverse people are. There is no use in struggling when we already have one foot in the grave. And we must not forgive and forget. We must

---

[9] Louis-Ferdinand Céline (1894–1961)—French writer who wrote extensively about fascism.

report, one by one, everything we have learned about the cruelty of man. Otherwise, we cannot die. If we do this, then our lives will not have been wasted.

People who continue to live in Hiroshima, instead of keeping silent or forgetting about the extreme tragedy of human history, are trying to speak about it, study it, and record it. It is a formidable task, calling for extraordinary effort. Outsiders can hardly comprehend the scope and intensity of the Hiroshima people's feelings—including the personal aversion to public exposure which they must conquer in order to carry out this task. The people who stick by the city are the only ones with a right to forget it and keep silent about it; but they are the very ones who choose to discuss, study, and record it energetically.

The women of the "Rivers of Hiroshima" series, the **advocates**[10] of the A-bomb white paper, the doctors of the A-bomb Hospital, and all the victims who ever talked about their own bitter experiences and about the Hiroshima within themselves—how modest and restrained they are in making their testimony. It is by no means strange that all these Hiroshima people should possess an unmistakable dignity. Only through lives like theirs do dignified people emerge in our society.

Not since I first felt, as a child, the dilemma of how to achieve dignity have I ever attempted to write, even for practice, an essay to resolve the issue. But I think that I have learned one sure way to protect myself from feeling shame or humiliation. And that way is to **endeavor**[11] never to lose sight of the dignity of people in Hiroshima.

---

[10] **advocates**—those who write or speak publicly in favor of; those who recommend publically a position or idea.

[11] **endeavor**—an earnest attempt or effort.

QUESTIONS TO CONSIDER

1. Why, according to Oe, do people seem to forget what happened at Hiroshima?

2. What does Oe find objectionable about the runner at the Olympic Games? How does his view differ from that of the American journalist?

3. Why does Oe believe that, in Céline's words, "The ultimate defeat is, in short, to forget"?

At the Bomb Testing Site

BY WILLIAM STAFFORD

William Stafford (1914–) is a poet who is famous as a teacher
and inspirer of other poets. His own poetry is generally about
contemplation and the hidden significance of events. "At the Bomb
Testing Site" occurs at the so-called Trinity site in the New
Mexican desert where the first atomic device was exploded in July
1945. Stafford was a conscientious objector during World War II.

At noon in the desert a **panting**[1] lizard
waited for history, its elbows tense,
watching the curve of a particular road
as if something might happen.

---

[1] **panting**—breathing hard, longing eagerly, yearning.

It was looking at something farther off
than people could see, an important scene
acted in stone for little selves
at the **flute**[2] end of consequences.

There was just a continent without much on it
under a sky that never cared less.
Ready for a change, the elbows waited.
The hands gripped hard on the desert.

---

[2] **flute**—long, pointed.

QUESTIONS TO CONSIDER

1. How would you describe the tone of this poem?

2. What is the "continent without much on it"?

3. What is the "change" referred to in line 11?
   How does Stafford view it?

Early Morning Test Light over Nevada, 1955

BY ROBERT VASQUEZ

Vasquez's poem originally appeared in New Voices, 1979-1983, *published in 1984 by the Academy of American Poets. It is representative of the reflections on the times when the first nuclear bombs were exploded.*

Your mother slept through it all,
her face turned away
like the dark side of the earth.

We'd heard
between *rancheras* on the radio
that the **ladles**[1]

---

[1] **ladles**—large, cup-shaped spoons.

and the two bears
that lie among the stars
above Nevada
would fade at 3:15 as though seared
by a false sun.

The stove exhaled all night
a **trinity**[2] of blue rings. You entered
your fourth month
of floating in the tropical,
star-crossed water
your mother carried under her heart
that opens and closes
like a butterfly.

When the sky flared,
our room lit up. Cobwebs
sparkled on the walls, and a spider
absorbed the light
like a **chameleon**[3] and began
to inch toward the outer rings
as if a fly trembled.

Roosters crowed. The dog
scratched at the door. I went outside
hearing the hens and thought *weasel*
and found broken eggs, the chicks
spongy, their eyes
stunned and shrouded
by thin veils of skin.

---

[2] **trinity**—group of three.
[3] **chameleon**—lizard that can change color to blend in with
its surroundings.

"Don't open your eyes,"
I whispered to you when darkness
returned. I thought of your bones
still a white gel, I remembered the story
of blood smeared on doorways,[4]
and I placed my hand on the balloon
you rode in—that would slowly sink
to your birth. I said
the Old German name your mother already picked
for you, *Robert*. It means *bright fame*.

---

[4] blood smeared on doorways—reference to the biblical story of Passover, where the angel of death who had come for each family in Egypt's eldest son skipped over the households that had blood smeared over their doorways.

QUESTIONS TO CONSIDER

1. What is the situation and who are the characters in the poem?

2. What is the irony of the choice of Robert for the soon-to-be-born son's name?

3. How does Vasquez feel about the impending birth of his son?

The Shadow

BY TŌGE SANKICHI

The Japanese poet Tōge Sankichi was a survivor of the atomic bombing of Hiroshima, though in the end he died of medical complications stemming from his exposure to the radiation and explosion. Tōge was active in the postwar era in trying to create a Japan that would never again be the cause of a war. His poems are part of the Japanese conscience about the war and the terrible destruction in both Hiroshima and Nagasaki. "The Shadow" describes postwar Hiroshima with great irony.

Cheap movie theaters, saloons, fly-by-night
   markets,
burned, rebuilt, standing, crumbling, spreading like
   the itch—
the new Hiroshima,
head shiny with hair oil,
barefaced in its **resurgence**;[1]

---

resurgence—rising again.

already visible all over the place,
in growing numbers, billboards in English;
one of these: "Historic A-Bomb Site."
Enclosed by a painted fence
on a corner of the bank steps,
stained onto the grain of the dark red stone:
a quiet pattern.

That morning
a flash tens of thousands of degrees hot
burned it all of a sudden onto the thick slab of granite:
someone's trunk.

Burned onto the step, cracked and watery red,
the mark of the blood that flowed as intestines melted
    to mush:
a shadow.

Ah! If you are from Hiroshima
and on that morning,
amid indescribable flash and heat and smoke,
were buffeted in the whirlpool of the glare of the
    flames, the shadow of the cloud,
crawled about dragging skin that was peeling off,
so transformed that even your wife and children
would not have known you,
this shadow
is etched in tragic memory
and will never fade.

Right beside the street where the people of the city
    come and go,
well-meaning but utterly indifferent,
assaulted by the sun, attacked by the rain, covered over
    by dust,
growing fainter year by year: this shadow.
The bank with the "Historic Site" sign at the foot of

the steps
dumped out into the street pieces of stone and glass, burned
    gritty,
completed a major reconstruction,
and set the whole enormous building sparkling in the evening
    sun.
In the vacant lot diagonally across.
drawing a crowd: a quack in the garb of a mountain
    ascetic.[2]

Indifferent, the authorities say: "If we don't protect it
    with glass or something,
it will fade away," but do nothing.
Today, too,
foreign sailors amble up in their white leggings,
come to a stop with a click of their heels,
and, each having taken a snapshot, go off;
the shoeshine boy who followed them here
peers over the fence, wonders why all the fuss,
and goes on his way.

---

[2] **ascetic**—person who practices unusual self-denial and restraint, often from ordinary pleasures and comforts.

QUESTIONS TO CONSIDER

1. What is the shadow described in the poem? Is it the same shadow as in the title?

2. What does the shoeshine boy represent to Tōge?

3. What do you think is Tōge's message about the bombing and its importance? What are Tōge's feelings about postwar events?

ACKNOWLEDGEMENTS

14 The ABC of the Atom. "The ABC of the Atom," by J. Bronowski from *Hiroshima Plus 20,* Delacorte Press, Copyright 1945, 1951, 1963, 1964, 1965 by The New York Times. Reprinted by permission.

24 The Creator of the Bomb: Oppenheimer Portfolio. Reprinted with the permission of Scribner, a Division of Simon & Schuster from *Oppenheimer* by I. I. Rabi, Robert Serber, Victor F. Weisskopf, Abraham Pais, and Glenn T. Seaborg. Copyright © 1969 by Charles Scribner's Sons.

24 The Creator of the Bomb: Hans Bethe. Reprinted with the permission of Simon & Schuster from *The Making of the Atomic Bomb* by Richard Rhodes. Copyright © 1986 by Richard Rhodes.

24 The Creator of the Bomb: Oppenheimer on the Trinity Test. From *The Decision to Drop the Bomb,* Giovannitti and Freed, Coward-McCann, 1965.

24 The Creator of the Bomb: Oppenheimer in His Speech. From *Robert Oppenheimer Letters and Recollections,* edited by Alice Kimball Smith and Charles Weiner, Harvard University Press, 1980, pp. 315-325. Reprinted by permission of Stuart Smith.

32 Potsdam July 25. "Diary (Potsdam) July 25, 1945" by Harry S. Truman. Reprinted by permission of Ann Elmo Agency, Inc. From the book *Off the Record: The Private Papers of Harry S. Truman.* Copyright © Robert H. Ferrell, 1980.

40 The Decision to Use the Atomic Bomb. "The Decision To Use The Atomic Bomb" by Henry L. Stimson. Copyright © 1947 by Harper's Magazine. All rights reserved. Reproduced from the February issue by special permission.

59 Thank God for the Atomic Bomb. From *Thank God for the Atom Bomb and Other Essays* by Paul Fussell, Summit Books, 1988. © 1988 Paul Fussell. Reprinted by permission.

67 Akira Miuri and John Kenneth Galbraith. From *The Good War* by Studs Terkel. Copyright © 1984 by Studs Terkel. Reprinted by permission of Donadio & Ashworth, Inc.

86 A White Light and Black Rain. "A White Light and a Black Rain" from *Seven Hours to Zero* by Joseph L. Marx, G. P. Putnam's Sons, 1967.

96 Injuries to the Human Body. From *Hiroshima and Nagasaki: The Physical, Medical and Social Effects of the Atomic Bombing* by Iwanami Shoten, Publishers. Reprinted by permission of Basic Books, a member of Perseus Books, L.L.C.

102 Hiroshima: The Victims. From *No High Ground* by Fletcher Knebel. Copyright © 1960 by Fletcher Knebel and Charles W. Bailey III, renewed © 1988 by Fletcher Knebel and Charles W. Bailey III. Reprinted by permission of HarperCollins Publishers, Inc.

117 From Hiroshima. From *Hiroshima* by John Hersey. Copyright 1946 and renewed 1974 by John Hersey. Reprinted by permission of Alfred A. Knopf, Inc.

121 from Children of the A-Bomb. From *Children of the A-Bomb: The Testament of the Boys and Girls of Hiroshima* compiled by Dr. Arata Osada. Translated by Jean Dan and Ruth Sieben-Morgen, G.P. Putnam's Sons, 1959.

128 Voices of an A-Bomb Survivor. Interview of an A-Bomb survivor: Ms. Michiko Yamaoka by Mitsuru Ohba. Copyright © 1995. Used by permission of Mitsuru Ohba.

132 Atomic Bombing of Nagasaki. From "A Giant Pillar of Purple Fire" by William L. Laurence, September 9, 1945. Copyright © 1945 by The New York Times. Reprinted by permission.

152 Hiroshima: Historians Reassess. "Hiroshima: Historians Reassess" by Gar Alperovitz is reprinted in full text with permission from FOREIGN POLICY Magazine, Summer 1995, pp. 15-34. © 1995, Carnegie Endowment for International Peace.

161 Why America Dropped the Bomb. "Why America Dropped the Bomb" by Donald Kagan from *Commentary*. Copyright © September 1995. Reprinted by permission of Commentary and the author. All rights reserved.

176 The Scientists. "Scientists: Their Views 20 Years Later," by William L. Laurence from *Hiroshima Plus 20,* Delacorte Press, Copyright 1945, 1951, 1963, 1964, 1965 by the New York Times Company.

188 Smithsonian Scuttles Exhibit. "Smithsonian Scuttles Exhibit: Enola Gay Plan Had 'Fundamental Flaw'" by Eugene L. Meyer and Jacqueline Trescott, from *The Washington Post,* January 31, 1995. © 1995, The Washington Post. Reprinted with permission.

204 When the Vacation is Over for Good. "When the Vacation is Over for Good" from *Selected Poems by Mark Strand.* Copyright © 1979, 1980 by Mark Strand. Reprinted by permission of Alfred A. Knopf, Inc.

206 On Human Dignity. From *Hiroshima Notes* by Kenzaburo Oe, translated by David L. Swain and Toshi Yonezawa. Copyright © 1981 by David L. Swain and Toshi Yonezawa. Reprinted by permission of Marion Boyars Publishers, New York and London.

214 At the Bomb Testing Site. "At the Bomb Testing Site" copyright 1960, 1998 by the Estate of William Stafford. Reprinted from *The Way It Is: New & Selected Poems* by William Stafford with the permission of Graywolf Press, Saint Paul, Minnesota.

216 Early Morning Test Light. "Early Morning Test Light over Nevada, 1955," by Robert Vasquez, 1984. Originally appeared in *New Voices,* 1979-1983.

219 The Shadow. Sankichi, Toge, "The Shadow," from *Hiroshima: Three Witnesses.* Copyright © 1990 by Princeton University Press. Reprinted by permission of Princeton University Press.

Photo research: Diane Hamilton

Index